New Media Cultures

New Media Cultures

P. David Marshall

A member of the Hodder Headline Group
LONDON
Distributed in the United States of America
by Oxford University Press Inc., New York

ARNOLD

First published in Great Britain in 2004 by
Arnold, a member of the Hodder Headline Group,
338 Euston Road, London NW1 3BH

hht://www.arnoldpublishers.com

Distributed in the United States of America by
Oxford University Press Inc.
198 Madison Avenue, New York, NY10016

Hodder Headline's policy is to use papers that are natural, renewable and
recyclable products and made from wood grown in sustainable forests.
The logging and manufacturing processes are expected to conform to the
environmental regulations of the country of origin.

The advice and information in this book are believed to be true and
accurate at the date of going to press, but neither the author nor the publisher
can accept any legal responsibility or liability for any errors or omissions.

British Library Cataloguing in Publication Data
A catalogue record for this book is available from the Library of Congress

ISBN 0 340 80699 0

1 2 3 4 5 6 7 8 9 10

Typeset in 10/13pt Abode Garamond by Servis Filmsetting Ltd, Manchester
Printed and bound in Malta

What do you think about this book? Or any other Arnold title?
Please send your comments to feedback.arnold@hodder.co.uk

Contents

General editors' preface

Cultural studies is a rapidly developing field of pedagogical practice and theoretical enquiry. Among its distinctive characteristics is the way its influence has spread across disciplines and research areas. While the effect of cultural studies on a wide range of disciplinary or sub-disciplinary fields has been substantial and in some cases profound, most publication in the area is less interested in that influence than in mapping the current hierarchies of positions and knowledges seen to define the field. The work of definition and clarification has preoccupied cultural-studies publishing for most of its history. This series hopes to move forward by mapping the ways in which the approaches and politics of cultural studies have affected both the detail and the overall shape of work within the humanities and social sciences today. The series will produce textbooks which critically describe and assess the contribution of cultural studies to specific areas of research and debate.

John Storey and Graeme Turner

Acknowledgements

This book is fabricated from many threads. Those material threads intersect with a number of significant individuals who have assisted in making the ideas germinate and the writing unfold. I would like to thank Abigail Woodman, my editor at Hodder Arnold, for her patience and support. Graeme Turner has also been instrumental in the development of the idea for the book and making it part of the Cultural Studies in Practice series that he has edited.

The ideas in this book have been trialled in a variety of locations and circumstances. Talks given at Karlstad, MIT, Bergen, the University of Queensland, the University of Southern California and Northeastern University have been useful in developing the directions taken in this book more solidly and I thank those that have invited me. In addition, the students in my New Media Cultures course at Northeastern have assisted collectively in challenging and debating the approaches advanced in this book firsthand. My faculty and staff at Northeastern – particularly Alison Hearn, Murray Forman, Alan Zaremba, Michael Woodnick, Walter Carl, Joanne Morreale, Jayson Harsin, Carey Noland, Kristen Kilbashian and Angela Chin – have helped make the kind of collegial environment which aids in the research and writing process. I have had several research interns and assistants who also assisted in the completion of the project: Jessica Volpi, Michelle O'Berg, Joe Lubarski, Zeena Majali, Andrew Marshall and Lindsey Ganzer.

Finally, my family has once again toiled through the periods of distraction and anxiety that I unfailingly make an unwelcome partner in the writing process. Thank you Erin, Hannah and Isaac. And especially thank you Louise.

P. David Marshall
Nahant, Ma.
March 2004

Preface

This book investigates, from the vantage point of cultural theory and the viewpoint of the actual forms of the emerging cultures of new media. These cultures, in their dynamic relationship with products, networks, hardware, software and practices, are constantly changing in sometimes profound and sometimes banal ways. In order to capture that transformation, we have developed a website to accompany the material in this book. The contents of the website are designed to supplement the seven chapters of this book with further illustrative examples, critical questions and discussions that arise from each chapter's content, connections and links to further research and study, and some key areas that are primed by the chapters' material for investigation.

You can find the website at www.newmediacultures.co.uk, and you can use it in tandem with the book to explore new media cultures in even greater depth.

chapter one

Introduction: 'new media' and cultural studies

What's 'new' about new media?

I'm multi-tasking

Let's begin with a premise: with every change in the way we communicate in our culture there is a new struggle over meaning, significance, knowledge and power. Old rules and orders cannot be applied perfectly under the new regime of communication and thus formations of power are under threat from these new forms of expression. The premise here is not exactly a technological determinist argument; that is, it is not saying that technology determines culture. New forms of communication are only partially determined by their technology and are shaped from social and cultural conditions, and from the various manners in which cultural expression, and intentions are conveyed. Cultural forms, such as the novel, are part technology and part cultural expression, and their development is dependent on both cultural and technological conditions. For instance, the novel as a book is dependent on the technologies of mass reproduction, mass printing and mass distribution; but the novel is also dependent on a cultural development of story-telling that allowed it to be expressed in narrative form, the expansion of literacy, and the emergence of printing in vernacular languages. Moreover, the book was equally dependent on the emergence of an industrial economy and the development of copyright. All of these technological, cultural and economic factors – along with a host of others that I have glossed over in my analysis – are embedded in the cultural formation of the novel and its emergence in the eighteenth century. Nonetheless, the emergence of the novel was a challenge to existing structures of both knowledge and power. In its time it was a new media form that led to a struggle over meaning, significance, knowledge and power.

This book is an investigation of the struggle over meaning, significance, knowledge and power produced by what have been dubbed 'new media' in contemporary culture. Because of the massive amount of hype that has surrounded new media and our own culture's fascination with the new, it is worth questioning whether these 'new media' are in fact anything new. There is a potential barrage of other questions that arise once we investigate what new actually means, and then a further flurry of questions when we analyse that idea of the new in the context of media and media forms. In this book, the newness of new media, even as what is really new and what is just a reformation of what already exists is contested, represents a challenge to some of our ways of analysing media and, at the very least, gives us an opportunity to think through whether our use of media now is shifting and changing the way we relate to it. In other words, what we are working through here, is whether there is a change in the culture that is related to these new media forms. Can we make the claim that there are new media cultures developing that may have affinities to past media and the way we used them, but identify shifts and ruptures that deserve both greater scrutiny and may point to new cultural struggles?

To begin this analysis of new media we need to isolate some of the key differentiations between new and old. From that vantage point we can identify those of greatest significance. Old and new are relational terms and not absolutes. It is somewhat arbitrary therefore to delineate the old from the new. Nonetheless, it is useful to look at both older and newer forms of media:

Printed Forms → → → → → → → → letters, books, newspaper, magazines	Printed Forms The Internet, The World Wide Web, email, palm pilots, mobile phones, digital television graphics
Images → → → → → → → → → → photographs, film, television	Images DVDs, digital cinema, satellite television, Digital photography, the Web, Internet, mobile telephones, web cams, replay television
Sound → → → → → → → → → → → → phonograph, telephone, radio	Sound Ipods, MP3s, mobile telephones, web radio, digital cable music

In this arbitrary analytical breakdown, one of the most interesting points to emerge is that media was much more clearly delineated in its older forms. In our categories of transformation, particular media forms appear and reappear. For instance, the internet and the web now constitute all these media forms. Web pages are usually a form of printed text. Contained in those web pages, however, are digital images and moving images. Music and sounds are also central to the web and the internet as music is downloaded on computers or other more portable listening devices. Thus my first point about new media is that the former distinctions no longer make sense in terms of the site or physical location of media. Printed media blends into other media; visual media is not isolated in its delivery systems of television and film exhibition. The distinctions may still play in how people use media forms, but in terms of the technological forms there is a blurring of the machines of reproduction and dissemination.

What insights can be drawn from this confluence of media forms into something new? It is important to recognize that this convergence has not developed from some natural evolution. It is derived from many interests and many competing claims that seek to define what constitutes our media.

Think for a moment about how television is defined. We readily think of the genres of television, from news and sitcoms, to dramas and exhibition of films. We also think now of the various channels devoted to particular generic programmes. Television as a technology, however, does not need to be organized in this way. Television's current constitution is an amalgam of particular economic, cultural and political interests and decisions. In the North American context, it has been organized around private networks that have helped shape later satellite and cable-delivered networks. As we are very aware, advertising has been instrumental in organizing television's content and its economy. But this did not necessarily have to be the case and other competing models of television delivery were developed in other parts of the world. In the middle of the twentieth century, television was conceptualized as a form of two-way communication much like the telephone and also much like early versions of radio. In most of Europe and Asia, television was first conceptualized as a government-controlled public system. Depending on the political system, such a television system was either an organ of the government or was seen as an independent voice in the public sphere.

What appeared on television in any of these systems generally had to go through an elaborate gatekeeping process. Apart from local access programming, television was seen to be expensive and there was a drive to maintain a distinction of what was deemed 'broadcast quality' in its programmes. Once again, the decisions around what was included and excluded from television have been significant and have been motivated by particular and powerful interests. Yet television is a principal way in which any culture expresses its stories to its people; television is a form of re-presentation and re-articulation of the culture, however much it is fabricated and constructed into genres and fictions. How those stories of re-presentation are told, who is permitted to tell and which stories are told explains a great deal about a culture and the forms of power within that culture. Commercial television is constrained in its re-presentation of a culture so as not to offend the corporations that sponsor the programming. This commercial imperative therefore shapes the kind of television that we see and the way that stories are told.

Although television as a cultural form transforms as it attempts to accommodate different interests and developments in a culture, it has developed a recognizable pattern of producing content and responding to its audience. The question that needs to be answered is: do new media forms produce both distinctively different content and 'audiences' when compared with their predecessors? The answer to this question is a qualified yes. It is important to realize that one of the developments of our new media is that they have appropriated some of the qualities and relationships from past media forms. For instance, videogames are played through a television and in some ways they are an expansion of the uses made of television. Television's primacy of location in the house, in the lounge and the living room, created interesting familial conflicts of use over the last 20 years as videogames became a more prevalent use of television. The emergence of videogames more or less coincided with the development of multiple television sets in middle-class homes. The correlation between multiple set ownership and the expansion of the videogame industry makes one realize the sometimes connected interests of apparently different and competing media forms. Nonetheless, a new media form such as the videogame implies quite different forms of production and reception than television does, which makes it qualitatively different and distinctive from television. In chapter five, we will explore these dimensions of difference further; suffice to say that the videogame is non-narrative, often recursive in its gameplay and has a fundamentally different production process than most television.

Other media forms have varying degrees of differentiation from their past as these forms have incorporated the past's content. The internet in its various guises envelopes a great deal of content, media production and consumption patterns from the past. Letters have an affinity with email; instant messaging with its abbreviated language form harks back to telegraph short-forms; the web itself graphically implies magazines and newspapers; lists, weblogs, webcams and personal websites reinvigorate the newsletter, the diary and other efforts at producing more private forms of communication for a wider public.

Newer media often imply a supersession of the older form; but it should be made clear that new media have not historically obliterated their past. Many futurists imagined television spelling the end of radio and this has been replicated with the internet somehow superseding newspapers. The more complicated reality is that media forms change when newer forms appear and there is a different accommodation of a media mix. With the introduction of television, for instance, the older media form, radio, became much more focused on environments where television was unlikely to be watched. Radio became less significant in the household, but incredibly more significant in cars and in public places such as beaches or parks. Radio's genres of programmes also shifted as it became much more about being an ambient cultural form rather than calling for concentrated attention. Progressively, radio became about either talk, news or music. Gradually television assumed much of the rest of the entertainment programmes that radio once broadcast. Thus television inherited genres from radio such as the crime drama or the situation comedy or the daily soap opera.

In our investigation of new media, it is important to develop a sensitivity and sensibility to media transformations. For instance, fewer people may write letters, but this hasn't eliminated the letter, the postcard or the greeting card as means of communication. Cultural activities associated with media forms are complex in the way that they connect with people and communities. A worthwhile study of new media must develop how the medium conveys, expresses, enables and helps constitute cultural activities and communities. It cannot presume that technology immediately transforms; at the same time a study of new media must be aware that something significantly different and new can emerge from the relationship between the uses of old media and new media.

The adaptability of the mass communication tradition to new media

To unravel the intricate relationship between a new media form and the way it intersects with and develops cultural activities, it is useful to adapt past approaches that have been particularly successful at understanding media and cultural forms. There are several traditions that have studied media intensively that may be valuable to new media investigations. One of these is **mass communication research**, which has been derived mainly from the field of sociology. This tradition has been particularly powerful in three directions: within the media industries themselves; in the development of critical study of media; and in the formulation of government policy related to media. Although mass communication research has many variations, it is fundamentally a quantitative analysis technique for the study of media forms. In its development, its form of quantitative analysis has taken two clear trajectories. First of all, since the 1930s, some form of mass communication research has investigated the audience by providing aggregated statistics about what people watch, read and listen to. One could say that this type of mass communication research has served the industry. Its most sophisticated industry representative is the Company ACNeilsen which operates in over 30 countries gathering as much information about audiences as possible. Its clients are radio and television stations, networks and the many advertisers that work to strategically place their messages to maximize their reach with a core audience via these various media networks. Political polling and market research are the sister industries of this type of mass communication research. All of them are derived from statistical studies that were part of the national census programmes that map the make-up of any country and have been developing in their sophistication since the late nineteenth century. Mass communication audience research works in sophisticated ways to determine the demographic profile of an audience. This kind of research has migrated naturally into the study of new media. One can find that ACNielsen's Mediametrix, along with a number of other providers, attempts to chart the use of the internet. They, once again, are servicing the relationship between media entities and advertisers so that appropriate rates can be applied for the placement of an advertisement. Similar services chart the use of online and videogames where the industry objective is to monitor taste preferences of their players and to modify their future products to reflect or capture these audiences more completely.

The second type of quantitative research undertaken from a mass communication perspective is content analysis. Many studies have attempted to determine the frequency of certain images or words in any given text. One of the most common forms of content analysis is the analysis of news: how frequently are certain issues presented in the news, how often is a certain word used to describe a given situation and what stories dominate the television evening news are all types of question that lead researchers to analyse the content of a particular media form. Essentially what is being investigated is the bias or general tendency of the news and press. Other forms of content analysis have different objectives. For instance, many studies have looked at the regularity of the depiction of violence on television or in films. George Gerbner's studies over the last three decades have compared the difference between the television world of violence and the real world of violence in American culture. His research has discovered that television massively over-represents the potential of violence and crime in society, and he has developed what he calls a cultivation thesis to explain how this misrepresentation skews Americans to fear their everyday world (Gerbner, 1988). Counting depictions of sex and violence has produced the greatest number of media-related research surveys that have used content analysis. In its nascent form, new media has also been investigated for its frequency of certain words and images. Countless surveys claim that sex is the most common word put into a search engine. Other research has attempted to provide content analysis of chatrooms while there has been further studies on how the news is presented online. Although in a much more qualitative manner, content analysis is the basis of the many viewing codes on films as much as video and computer games.

From these two trajectories, a third variation of this research has developed – **effects research**. Since the 1960s, many mass communication researchers have attempted to study the effects of exposure to particular types of media content. Effects research is less derived from sociology than from psychology and its object of investigation is often violence and the media. Partly motivated by trying to provide a causal relationship between media use and violent acts, effects research has garnered the greatest amount of government research monies compared to any other research that has studied the media. Effects research is often done in controlled or laboratory environments where test subjects are exposed to particular types of violent programming and then studied for behavioural changes. Children are often the focus of these studies. Effects research has developed a higher degree of sophistication when employed in the advertising industry. Fundamentally, this research is attempting to quantify emotional, behavioural and attitudinal changes in an audience, which can be directly related to a particular media stimulus. Different new media have been similarly investigated, but none more so than videogames and the effect of their violent content.

Generally, the mass communication research tradition has incompletely understood the role of media within a culture and has often misunderstood in its aggregations how media operate in their ordinary and everyday usage. Mass communication research can form a quantitative base for understanding the nature of media in a culture, but it demands more qualitative investigations of audience use and meaning-making. It is the kind of research that allows studies of the media to speak in the language of science or at least in the language of social science. This is a powerful discourse within a culture, and stories of the effects of videogames or of the internet rival the readings of the effects of television and circulate widely through the media and government.

A slightly divergent tradition has emerged from the social sciences and effects research. It is an approach that has looked at the predispositions of people to particular media use and how people try to match those desires to the programmes that are on offer from the media. This tradition, which grew from American media functionalism as championed by Paul Lazarsfeld and expanded by researchers such as Blumler, has generally been called the uses and gratifications research model (Katz and Lazarsfeld, 1955; Blumler and Katz, 1974). Still relying to some degree on psychology, uses and gratifications has studied how people match up their media use to their lives, their moods, their behaviours and, in some cases, to other people who are influential in their lives. Because the approach identifies the very power of the individual to determine their desires and to act on them, it is generally a model that fits into the main tenets of consumer culture as well as the structure of the commercialized media industry. With the individual having ultimate sovereignty over a range of choices and possibilities, it allows media corporations to slip the knot of responsibility for their content and their programming: the media consumer ultimately makes the choice as to what is shown and presented.

The cultural studies tradition and the value of the active audience approach

Of all the more traditional mass communication research approaches to the media, uses and gratifications research actually has the greatest applicability in the era of new media forms. Its weakness, however, is its inability to deal with the social, economic and cultural structures that shape the media that we use, even in the media's new incarnations. Another approach to studying the media has emerged from the intellectual tradition of cultural studies which, in a very fundamental way, deals with what uses and gratifications studies does well, but also deals with what is lacking and overlooked in much of the rest of mass communication research.

The cultural studies approach to the media decentres what has been privileged in traditional mass communication research. To begin with, it deconstructs the notion of the 'mass'. The concept of the mass implies that there is something unifying and unitary about how people act. It is an approach to the study of contemporary society that developed from nineteenth-century sociology and has an implicit negative critique of what emerges from the crowd or the mass. The mass is alienated, anonymous and of lower value than privileged individual thinking and action (Swingewood, 1974; Arnold, 1994). The mass has always been interpreted as dangerous and unstable, and always a group that is 'other' than the people labelling. In common criticism of television that comes from this 'critique of the mass' tradition, we often hear it said that television panders to 'the lowest common denominator'. What is made explicit here is that television presents the weakest thoughts of our culture, not its best. So mass society research, where mass communication research is a powerful research subset, has its origins predominantly from this critique of the mass.

Cultural studies' starting point is to make the claim that the mass is a myth that is deployed for particular ends. For the industry, it simplifies the conceptualization of the audience into aggregates. For the conservative critics of contemporary culture, it is shorthand for dismissing the activities of most of the population without serious study. What is distinctive about the cultural studies approach is that it investigates new formations of social and cultural categories more completely. Drawing from Marxism, cultural studies provides a pattern for investigating cultural transformations reconstructed by the subordinate classes of society, as well as identifying and comprehending how the dominant classes try to maintain their position of dominance. The key feature of cultural studies that differentiates it from more orthodox Marxist approaches is that it privileges cultural activity as a place of significant contestation within a particular culture. More orthodox Marxist approaches would claim that this world of ideas is dominated by the ruling classes' ideas and where active change can occur is at the level of production and labour. In other words, media produce an ideology of how the culture should and does operate that is in concert with the dominant ruling elite and works to maintain that order. The cultural studies perspective challenges this reading in two ways. First, it identifies cultural activity as a means through which subordinate groups construct their identity. The media and its messages, instead of articulating the endpoint of meaning, represent the starting point for the production of meaning in a culture. Media is the raw material for a process of making meaning that is remade to make sense within the particular cultural setting. Second, cultural studies underlines that the process of making meaning is politically significant as it works to shift and challenge the organization of cultural power as much as it coalesces identity in subordinate culture (see Turner, 2002).

This kind of thinking about the role of media in culture that cultural studies provides has produced an enriching source for interpreting traditional media. In contradistinction to the idea of the passive television viewer, cultural studies underlines the activity of the audience. Reception, of whatever media form, is a kind of work, a cultural production. Integrated into this approach is the significant interpretive concept of hegemony. Hegemony, originally developed by Antonio Gramsci, is a term that identifies that there is an active building of consent and consensus by the dominant class (Bocock, 1986). One of the most interesting locations for building and winning the consent of the wider populace is through the media. The popularity of television programmes, the success of a genre of popular music or a blockbuster film, identify this complex work of hegemony. On the one hand, the media industry is trying to produce a hit and is manufacturing the particular cultural form in order for it to appeal to the populace – that is, it is providing a cultural form that does not challenge the existing structure. The reality is that in order for the film to appeal it has to have qualities that resonate with the population in some way. The audience of a film or a television programme gets some pleasure from the production, and that pleasure identifies the working hegemony that is in operation in the constant appeal of media forms to attract an audience. In the industry's appeal to attract an audience, the meaning and message cross over somewhat in the direction of the audience's collective pleasure. Hegemony, then, expresses how domination continues, but underlines how subordinate messages are incorporated as consensus is built and maintained.

The value of the cultural studies approach to the analysis of traditional media is best understood through some examples. Many studies have looked at popular music and the uses made of the form in particular settings. Hebdige's study of British youth subculture in the 1970s identified how disenfranchised working-class youths were instrumentally part of the remaking of popular music into punk. Their bodies became the source for the expression of their difference and the solidarity of their experience of difference. Musical form and sartorial style were both political and cultural statements that were articulated in the garb of everyday actions and not by the perceived-to-be politically active (Hebdige, 1988). Lawrence Grossberg's use of American popular music to describe the political and cultural landscape of the 1980s similarly articulated the way that popular music can be deployed and express oppositional meanings as much as hegemonic meanings (Grossberg, 1992). Ien Ang's re-reading of the television audience identified the plurality of audiences as opposed to the more uni-dimensional audience that was bought and sold in the industry (Ang, 1991). Henry Jenkins' research on fan cultures indicated that television programmes became the starting point for elaborate shared fantasies of committed fans to programmes such as *Star Trek* or *Dr Who* (Jenkins, 1992; Tulloch and Jenkins, 1995). Graeme Turner's classic re-reading of film underlines the way that films become meaningful beyond the industry's conceptualization, and further into the particularities and intersections of cultural experience and pleasures (Turner, 1999). John Hartley's reading of the practices of television celebrates the audience member's uses that they make of television (Hartley, 1992).

All of these examples focus on the activity of reception, or what we can call the active audience. John Fiske in his many books and articles perhaps best represents this tradition of media and cultural studies and its interpretation of the audience. The active audience approach is the direct challenge to the belief in the passivity of media audiences and the static nature of media texts (Fiske, 1996). In his study of reception, he identified a number of directions that are useful to hold on to as we move towards understanding new media. First of all, Fiske analysed the intertextuality in media and how this produced a kind of 'semiotic excess' of any text (Fiske, 1989). All media texts may have had their preferred meanings, but they also offered other possible interpretations that were in negotiation with this preferred reading. Depending on the cultural group, these negotiated relationships with the programme produced a different interpretation of the text itself. Others have investigated this semiotic excess further. Richard Dyer's investigation of the alternative interpretations of singer and film star Judy Garland by the gay subculture underlines the multiple meanings that can be derived from the same popular cultural texts (Dyer, 1986). Similarly, Kylie Minogue is read quite differently, from gay icon to pop star, in contemporary popular culture. Fiske's work explored the nature of popular culture and in that more general study he adapted de Certeau's concept of strategic and tactical interventions in the everyday life. For Fiske, all cultural forms produced through the elaborate apparatus of the various cultural industries lead to an audience in the 'art of making do' (Fiske, 1989: 4). What Fiske means by this expression is that the television programmes or other cultural forms do no quite express one's own cultural reality; nonetheless we appropriate these into our everyday lives, making them meaningful in some way.

The 'art of making do', from Fiske's conceptualization, is a celebration of the audience's work in transformation as it challenges the conventions of the passive audience; but contained in the idea of 'making do' is an acceptance of the ideological boundaries of one's activities and a sense of a level of resignation and lament. Although those boundaries are malleable by an audience, they are nevertheless the constrained materials through which people make sense of their lives. The lament underscores the power imbalances present in contemporary culture and how those imbalances lead to the kinds of cultural product that we see on television, read in magazines and hear on radio.

What makes Fiske's active audience thesis powerful is what others have developed around the productivity of that activity. In particular, those who have studied popular music have pointed to the cyclical nature of innovation that relies on the audience's appropriation of music and their efforts at revitalization. As an audience 'appropriates' a particular musical form in its transformation to make it meaningful for a particular subculture, it changes and in effect 'revitalizes' the music and its cultural significance through those changes into something qualitatively new but also valuable to the subculture and its identity. The industry, in turn, takes that revitalized cultural activity and appropriates it for its own process of revitalization and innovation of its musical product and sells it more widely as a commodity. Thus subcultures, from Rastafarians, to hip-hop culture, from punk or gay dance cultures to technoravers, become the sources for cultural innovation of the culture industries. Fashion as much as music relies on subcultural identities and their process of revitalizing their cultural practices as a source for renewing the ever changing look and surface structure of consumer culture.

Transforming cultural studies to look at new media: from consumption to production and the cultural production thesis

Cultural studies has provided a very useful way of reconceptualizing the nature of media consumption. The active audience thesis helps us explicate the complex interplay and negotiation between audience and production that is at the heart of contemporary culture. It accentuates that embedded in production is the process and meaning of consumption or reception. In many ways, cultural studies' reading of media successfully and quite appropriately breaks down the distinction between production and consumption. In other words, viewing a television programme or listening to music is a form of production as the viewer or listener interprets and makes sense of the cultural form. Some have called this a kind of productive consumption, which accentuates the productive elements of the consumption process.

As we will discover throughout this book, new media as cultural forms further challenge the divides between production and consumption, and in some cases makes the distinction meaningless. What I want to do here is to develop an approach that can identify the changes in cultural practices that have been part of the emergence of new media and adapt the cultural studies model for the study of media for this new cultural environment.

If we think once again of Fiske's concept of the 'art of making do' with all its nuance of transforming as much as living within the ideological constraints of contemporary cultural production, we can identify that resignation quality in the phrase as much as its celebration of tactical methods of resisting dominant culture. What we'd like to develop here is that the 'art of making do' also identifies the desire to actually 'make' cultural forms. Where cultural studies has very successfully identified the moments of transformation in cultural consumption, it also identifies this repressed desire to be part of cultural production and not just reception. Cultural studies' focus on reception then expresses two important points as we work to retool its approach for the study of new media cultures:

1. In the spectrum from production to consumption, the starting point for cultural studies is generally consumption.
2. The focus on consumption has successfully identified a kind of repression and transformation approach to media and culture: the repression can be summarized as a repressed desire to produce that is articulated through the audience re-making and re-forming cultural forms.

The challenge of new media to this approach is that they demand that we look at the process of production and work more closely and develop a new analytical starting point in this spectrum from production to consumption. This book endeavours to explore from a cultural studies perspective how new media make us engage more directly with production even as we study consumption. From the internet to the ways that mobile phones are used, from games to chatrooms, new media implies a changed spectrum of what defines production and what defines consumption. Similarly the new media industries, are working out the new parameters of cultural forms and how they can successfully determine at what point in this production process they can demand some money from users/audiences. In many ways, the traditional cultural studies approach, where the audience appropriates the cultural form, identifies the very centre of what is attractive about new media: they are cultural forms that have expanded the capacity for the viewer/user to produce. As the industry grapples with this new paradigm through copyright and intellectual property debates, new media users continue to encroach on appropriating and making their cultural forms their own.

We can conceptualize this approach to the study of new media as the **cultural production thesis**. Where cultural studies in the past developed incredible skills in the critical reading of media, the cultural production thesis points us to study more closely the process of production and the way in which the populace is engaged in that process of cultural production. To make an analogy, media and cultural studies have tended to promote a readerly approach to critical investigation and developed our skills of media literacy; the cultural production thesis emphasizes that a writerly perspective must be incorporated to understand the processes of making that are elemental to the meanings and practices of new media forms.

Where do we go from here? New media cultures by chapter

As we explore the new dimensions of cultural production that have been foregrounded by the various new media, it becomes clear that different political and cultural struggles accompany these shifts. In each chapter, we shall explore these tectonic shifts in cultural practice and discuss how they are weaving different patterns of identity formation and collectivities, shifted industrial practices, and transformed conceptualizations of audiences.

The next two chapters try to map out further the wider nature of new media culture through several key concepts. In chapter two, we explore the meaning of interactivity, one of the defining elements of new media cultures, and debate its effect on transforming the traditional media category of the audience to the new media persona of the 'user'. Chapter three then investigates the technological sensorium of new media cultures. First the technology is interpreted as an elaborate apparatus that through different political and economic interests shapes and fosters new cultural connections and relations heretofore unseen. The chapter debates the types of inclusion promised in the technological forms and the patterns of exclusion that are inherent in contemporary digital culture. We delve into how new media has played with access via the new economies that have been circulating with the growth of new media. Networks imply connection; but that connection is developing towards a new politics and a new public sphere that is not necessarily all about access and is often principally about developing new hierarchies in an apparently more globalized public sphere.

The remaining chapters look specifically at the cultures that surround particular forms of new media. Chapter four addresses the manifold cultural transformations that have accompanied the development of the internet over the last 20 years. On one level, the internet has reconstructed many patterns of interpersonal communication and allowed new types of community to emerge and flourish. Activities in chatrooms, blogs and email of virtual (online) sex identify the transformed 'intimacy' of new media cultures. This new pervasive intimacy presents further evidence of new and unstable divisions between public and private spheres of communication. The chapter also investigates the World Wide Web as a multimedia form that has both absorbed many other media and also serviced in a promotional structure existing media such as television. Through a study of personal websites and the emergence of both webcams and weblogs, we shall see how the web has been a major channel for the democratization of cultural production and a location for the expression of the self in a form that can be disseminated publicly and narcissistically. Finally, the web is studied for how it has been instrumental in challenging the structures and power of the music industry: like the other traditional cultural industries, there is a serious challenge at play in new media cultures around intellectual property and the right of the music fan to appropriate cultural artefacts.

Chapter five studies game cultures both as a practice and industry, and expands on how new media cultures have shifted to a fascination and exploration of play, both within work and outside of its parameters. Through an historical, generic and identity analysis of both electronic games and the gamer, the chapter delves into game cultures and the new formations of community and identification they have fostered.

Chapters six and seven shift the focus to look at how new media cultures have changed some of the more established media forms. Chapter six investigates the rejuvenation of television in the digital era. With the expansion of viewer choice, the transformation of the technologies of reception and the integration of greater layers of information within the structure of the television screen, television has repositioned itself to incorporate some elements of new media. Reality television specifically is interpreted as an appeal to the cultural production desires of the audience that have been fostered in the era of interactivity. In chapter seven, film is investigated both in terms of its digitalization and in terms of an industry attempting to redefine its cultural experience for its audience.

The conclusion works to stitch together the intersecting weaves of the cultures of new media and presents the necessity for a shifted approach in media and cultural studies from its bedrock of reception towards a more intricate reading of cultural production with all its dialectical interplay between the construction of the cultural commodity form and its reconstruction and appropriation by the user.

New media culture represents a challenge to cultural politics-as-usual. It requires a close investigation of the new cultural landscape that has been fostered through its various forms. The book's conclusion delves into the nature of the new cultures and new politics that are now regularly and routinely a feature of contemporary culture, and summarizes the insight derived from our new media cultural studies approach that we have defined as the cultural production thesis.

chapter two

Forms of interactivity: the disappearance of the audience

What is the difference between active and interactive? The supposed distinction serves as a definition of new media – that is, the media form has some embedded notion of interactivity that transforms it from the relationship that traditional media forms have possessed. On superficial levels, the level of activity and engagement of someone reading a novel may be as high or higher than the claimed interactivity of the computer-game player. Although this claim of greater engagement and activity can be made on behalf of the non-interactive novel, interactivity implies some sort of transformative relationship between the user of the media and the media form itself. Encoded into new media is the capacity to transform the actual flow and presentation of the material itself. This transformative relationship is critical in understanding the difference between active and interactive, and also provides the perceived superiority of the interactive media environment over the active media environment.

Let's ponder the idea of activity and how it has been conceptualized in cultural studies of media. In the introductory chapter I indicated that the active audience thesis provided a useful starting point for understanding new media because it investigated the productive qualities of media consumption and reception. Active can be conceptualized in a variety of ways. It can imply an engaged fan audience or a music-inspired subculture, or simply a negotiated or perhaps ironic reading of a newscast. Thinking of the audience as active means that audience members 'work' on media texts. Where we can see this activity most pervasively represented by audiences is in their 'intertextual' work on media texts. Intertextuality acknowledges the presence in any media form of other texts. Those other texts help determine the interpretation and reading of the given text through comparisons of similarity and difference with other texts. Although these connections to other texts may be encoded by the producers of the text, they only become enacted through the audience's process of interpretation. The activity of the audience generally with traditional media is at the point of consumption or reception even as the activity begins to change the meanings of these terms into something productive.

Interactive implies some element that transcends what we have described here as activity, which can be useful to investigate the cultural shift in identity and subjectivity that is connected to new media. Unfortunately, the term interactivity has been overused by the new media industries in order to sell the distinctiveness and value of their new technologies to the point where interactivity seems to represent little more than hyperbole, hucksterism and hype. Nonetheless, interactivity can be a useful way to distinguish new media culture. In order to reclaim the term, it is perhaps useful to explore its various incarnations in usage and through that etymological tracing identify some of the unique qualities that have shifted.

The roots of the term 'interactivity' provides us with some interesting insights. It is easy for us to forget the routineness with which the verb 'interact' was once used. To interact simply meant to relate on multiple levels to others. It implied a kind of group dynamic that one would foster in the classroom or other meeting settings. Fundamentally, interactions were a more elaborated interpersonal form of communication. The *OED* defines interactive as simply 'influencing each other' and involves 'people working together'. Thus its most common usage prior to new media was connected to two areas: group psychology where new therapies were developed that expanded beyond the talking cure through interaction with others; and in education where the effort was to improve the learning experience. Interaction had the connotation that the exchange between people identified a further engagement and investment in what was being presented – in others words, participants would take a greater possession of the ideas talked about because they had exchanged and debated those ideas and made them at least partially their own.

It is important, then, to read the concept of interactivity as emerging very directly from the value of interpersonal communication. Embedded in the concept is also some sense of more egalitarian relations among participants. Interactivity, at least in its ideal form, represented something that displaced the authority of any discourse in its dispersion among a group, and in its appropriation and articulation by that group's members.

Another key usage of interaction has been in any field that has connected to environmental discourse. Interaction implied a sensitivity to an ecology of space and place. In architecture, building materials were chosen that made sense in terms of their environment and interacted appropriately in that space. Buildings themselves were seen as environments that people could use and which they could move through appropriately. Similarly, in theatre space, light and acoustics were designed to provide the right mix for the particular production. Interaction and interactivity as concepts were thus connected to something that was complete or at least holistically represented in its acknowledgement of the interplay of many elements in the constitution of any space. Ecology and systems theory would be drawn to expressing the inherent structure of an environment in complex patterns of interactivity.

These two terminological origins of interactivity are foundational in understanding why interactivity has been such a powerful metaphor for describing new media culture. Using interactivity is as much a reflection of the desire to reach or return to these states with new cultural technologies as it is a celebration of the new. Calling something interactive expresses a utopian conceit that this return can be achieved and possibly successfully attained in a better way than in the past.

In new media culture, these two usages, albeit transposed from environmental discourse and interpersonal communication, can be seen to manifest into two clear forms of interactivity. One form of interactivity relies on replicating the interpersonal and its value for the appropriation of meaning. New media forms that privilege this dimension provide greater connection to others; they also provide a greater sense of control and ownership of the cultural form. New media forms are thus modelled on providing the possibility of exchange and interplay. The second form of interactivity privileged in new media forms is their capacity to provide complete environments. The objective of these new media is a kind of immersive state. Virtual reality is the endgame of this ecological form of interactivity, where the individual becomes part of a complete system in a game or an environment. The greater objective is complete simulation within these environments where sight, touch, taste and smell are recreated within the new media form for the player or user.

A third direction in the development and use of interactivity was a kind of representation of difference from the forms of interaction that past media forms presented. In a simple one-upmanship, new media was a reaction to the limitations of its predecessors. Interactivity thus meant a greater connection to an audience, where the past radio or television form of interaction was indirect and through forms such as fan mail. New media's interaction was a continuous connection or at least the promise of continuous interactivity between source and audience. Interactivity thus expressed the breakdown of the broadcast model of the delivery of information. This third usage became prevalent in the hype of new media. Its promise of change and empowerment intersected with the audience's desire for greater control of its media forms.

Each of these kinds of interactivity usage has been deployed in the development of new media by both industry and users. Together, these three conceptualizations of interactivity point to a transformation in expectations in popular and media culture. From the vantage point of these three key terminological origins of interactivity, we can investigate how other authors have thought about the meaning and significance of interactivity.

With its overuse related to new media, interactivity lost some of its connection to its past meanings and began to represent the technological versions of interaction. As Espen Aarseth intones: 'To declare a system interactive is to endorse it with a magic power' (Aarseth, 1997). Many other theorists and writers agree that interactivity has become an ideological construct of the industry that has lost its empowering value. The actual term interactivity was more or less coined to describe new media, as previous derivations of the word such as interact and interactions were not as strongly associated with technology. Indeed, the *OED* added this definition of interactive, which identifies this shift in meaning to become a technical term in computing by 1967: 'Pertaining to or being a computer or other electronic device that allows a two-way flow of information between it and a user, responding immediately to the latter's input' (*OED*, 2002). The term interactivity remains outside of the dictionary despite its ubiquity in use. This has led many others to identify that interactivity refers primarily to the relationship and 'interface' between human and machine. There is a spectrum of levels of interactivity, but the ultimate form refers to complete simulation:

[A]n attribute or functionality, intentionally designed into man-made objects, physical, or virtual environments, characterized by the ability to sense accurately, then respond or react dynamically and intelligently to movement, gestures, expressions, or changes in human bodily or psychological states and intentions, changes in geographic location, changes in environmental condition, or any combination. Such dynamic intelligence may be achieved by the use of scripting or programming, embedded microcontrollers, sensors, GPS, haptics, and network connections to other systems and data. Ideas or concepts for new applications exhibiting interactivity are traditionally communicated to other people through user scenarios.

(Interactivity Consultants, 2003)

Over the last decade, there have been many efforts to define this new form of interactivity. For instance, the game designer Chris Crawford explains that interactivity has to be thought of more as a process than an object or an endpoint (Crawford, 2002). The investigations of interactivity in computer-mediated communications have generated some interesting insights. Writing in 1995, Rogers set as the objective with technology that interactivity must be seen as a goal: '[interactivity is] the degree to which participants in a communication process can exchange roles and have control over their mutual discourse' (Rogers, 1995: 314). Working out the new relations between human and machine led some writers to coin new terms that underlined the key differences between traditional media and new media forms. Goldsmith and O'Regan explain that we can no longer think of the viewer in the era of the internet: 'Interactivity, at some levels, transforms the relation between consumer and producer as the "viewer" is intimately involved in mixing or producing their screen media experience' (O'Regan and Goldsmith, 2002: 103). In their work on how new media 'remediate' existing media presentation, Bolter and Grusin explain that interactivity is essentially how new media continuously engage the person in making choices as to what they see and how they see it (2000: 29). Where looking at a film demands a continuity of viewing position, new media often demand that you make decisions about what you will see next. The immediacy with which the computer screen transforms to these decisions defines the distinctive quality of the interactive experience. Lev Manovich, while outlining the redundancy of the term 'interactive' because all computer–human communication is interactive, provides some nuanced readings of what interaction entails and attempts to theorize how this changes the actor who engages in new media. He wants to think beyond the simplicity and 'literal interpretation' (2001: 57) of interactivity being defined by the press of a button or a mouse-click to a new hyperlinked web page. These material objectifications of interactivity allow us to overlook the way in which these are not our own decisions but rather the links provided to us by someone else. To identify this difference Manovich explains: 'The cultural technologies of an industrial society – cinema and fashion – asked us to identify with someone else's bodily image. Interactive media ask us to identify with someone else's mental structure. If the cinema viewer, male and female, lusted after and tried to emulate the body of the movie star, the computer user is asked to follow the mental trajectory of the new media designer' (2001: 61).

One can discern that there is a clear dialectical tension that emerges from these attempts to comprehend interactivity in new media. On the one hand interactivity implies a form of empowerment of the player or user, where the individual gains a sense of control over the time and images with which they will engage. Moving from link to link on the web is indeterminate and unpredictable except by the user themselves. So the user has control. On the other hand, interactivity implies only apparent control. In reality the new media apparatus is highly structured and, through its very design, provides the range of possible choices in advance. Although very rich in providing sensory information, virtual reality, for example, is an entirely constructed environment where the possibilities are mapped out into patterns of engagement quite completely. To explore this tension further, it is worth thinking through the two faces of interactivity: control and freedom.

Control

One of the defining features of new media is its dependence on the technology of computers. No matter what new media form one contemplates, the computer chip, the microprocessor and computer languages are somehow at its core. These computer technologies have developed in a number of directions over time. Certainly the microchip has allowed for the miniaturization of the functions of computers and this has permitted the technology to be integrated into the design of many products. For example, the mobile phone is more than telephony in its capacity to store numbers and addresses, and in its ability to have simple games displayed on its screen precisely because of the integration of computer technology with telecommunications. Similarly, even the more elaborate remote controls of digital television or the new digital video recorders are reliant on computer-related hardware and software. The plethora of electronic toys such as Game Boys and electronic 'pets' can only have emerged from the expansion of use of computer-related technologies to new consumer uses. New media is therefore an extension of the uses made of computer technology into other consumer, information and entertainment domains.

The controlling aspect of new media is derived from this computer technology and how it works. First of all, it is important to understand that computers and their powers of computation are related to a reduction of information to basic units. At the core of the development of computers is this binary system of allocating meaning and significance. All computations are related to a series of ones and zeroes. They may be a very long string of ones and zeroes, but nonetheless everything that is placed into and through a computer is in effect transformed into ones and zeroes – a kind of elaborate switching device between off (0) and on (1). For example, your computer screen is composed of pixels, bascially small dots of light. Each of those pixels in terms of its colour constitution is defined by a code of 1s and 0s which define that colour. Every key stroke that you press on your keyboard is likewise defined into this code at its very base. Computers from their origin developed two capacities: the ability to store numbers in a memory and the ability to exercise a series of operations or commands on those codes to complete the computations. Computer languages that have developed over the last 50 years are ways to write, manipulate and read the code.

The reduction of all information to a binary code is called digitalization. One prominent form of digitalization, the process of converting sound and image into digital form, has transformed the video and music industries as their formerly standalone technologies have been absorbed into computers that can read and manipulate the content. The basis of media convergence that we associate with new media is the ability to convert all media forms into computer code. This conversion is into a digital message. Musical compact discs and film-related DVDs are the original products of this conversion. Current variations of the conversion are MP3 files for music and mpeg files for moving images.

The beauty of computers and their storage and computational capacity is that they can handle incredibly complex codes and codes upon codes of information. With the development of the microchip the storage of complex information no longer required the vast space of very large computers and, progressively, could be handled by more compact machines.

As we have mentioned, digitalization can only be read through codes and commands generated by computer programmers who can produce it through various computer 'languages'. The development of the 'software' that runs on the hardware of computers is thus generated code that builds layers of code to produce the graphic user interface we are used to seeing on computer screens. These layers of codes are a series of interrelated commands that make the programs actually run. These commands are likewise built on the same system of binary codes that are the basis of all computers and their work.

The programs generated are thus shaping, by their design, the way people use computers. It may not be obvious because of their complexity; nonetheless computer programs provide clear boundaries and borders for their users. These design boundaries can be thought of as very elaborate systems of control. Perhaps the best example to illustrate how computers are systems of control is people's use of videogames and computer games. Many games are quite complex, with multiple levels and possibilities. Ultimately, however, games as computer programs are designed with specific objectives and goals that cannot be changed by players. There may be a feeling of the power to manipulate and engage in the game as a player, but the basic parameters of the game are fixed. The feeling of interactivity is thus constructed and defined within a range of choices and boundaries.

Control is at the very core of how computers developed as a technology. Conceptually, computers can be thought of as 'smart machines' that exhibit some qualities of what researchers call artificial intelligence. Smart machines demonstrate two key elements:

1. they can act autonomously, and
2. they can interact with humans in an appropriate and useful way.

The integration of 'smart' behaviour is what differentiates old media fundamentally from new media. Our televisions are smarter because they can adjust the picture semi-autonomously to light conditions and they can interact through digital technology to an array of consumer desires via the remote control. Similarly our various appliances, such as heating and cooling systems, are 'smarter' because they can be programmed to adjust and modulate the temperature appropriately and regularly to the needs and conditions of a household.

The conceptual origins of 'smart' technology and computers is something called cybernetics. Cybernetics means simply a system of self-steering. Its history is connected to ballistics research from the Second World War, but it emerged contemporaneously in the fields of environmental science or ecology and systems theory in political and social sciences. The theoretical breakthrough associated with cybernetics can best be explained through ballistics. Researchers such as Norbert Wiener were faced with the problem that when people shot missiles at aeroplanes in the sky they missed too regularly. By the time the missiles reached their destination or target, the plane was no longer in the position aimed at. Wiener developed the idea of integrating the target, the missile and the missile launching into one interrelated system. If technology could be developed that linked the plane to the missile in some way so that when the plane changed course the missile would adjust accordingly, then more missiles would be launched successfully and more planes shot down. The objective or goal of the system was gruesome but simple: to have the plane and the missile meet. What was needed was a feedback system that allowed for information or 'communication' to occur between plane and missile. The nature of that information would work to adjust the missile to maintain the objective of the system (Wiener, 1948). Ultimately, ballistics research developed 'smart' missiles that had the ability to alter their course to match their target; we have seen them in use in both Gulf Wars. This cybernetic insight was not limited to missile research but became a way to model both the human and natural world into interrelated and interacting systems.

In cybernetics, any information generated was there to constrain the system towards its objectives. Simple cybernetic systems that demonstrate this constraint are devices such as thermostats, where any change in temperature from what is the norm or objective of the system leads to feedback that turns the heat on or off. When everything is on target, the system is described as in equilibrium or homeostasis.

Understanding cybernetics allows us to comprehend how the kind of interactivity developed by computers (which works on this cybernetic model) is really about integrating the person into the objectives of the system and conserving its outcomes. The cultures of new media mean living in this cybernetic world of control or, at the very least, the potential for control.

Let's go through a few examples to get further into the controlling quality of new media cultures.

Constant surveillance

One of the cultural conditions of new media cultures is that we are constantly surveyed and surveilled. The techniques of monitoring people have grown in their sophistication and their cybernetic feedback loops. For over 20 years, public and private spaces have had increasing numbers of video cameras. With their miniaturization through microchips, cameras can be located virtually anywhere. The performance cyber-artist Stellarc graphically demonstrated this in one of his works, where he allowed a miniature camera to explore his throat and stomach. In the more everyday world, the camera has become ubiquitous in its collection of information for feedback to control spaces. Because cameras can be more easily operated remotely, they can more effectively control spaces and report back to some central base for disciplinary action. One of the more interesting variations on camera use includes the nannycam to monitor the activities of baby-sitters while parents are not home. Web rings have been set up internationally to monitor the security of houses. Gated communities are models of the cybernetic world: their systems of surveillance ensure that the goals of the system are maintained while anything foreign or extraordinary to the system is treated as a kind of feedback that has to be eliminated. The effect of the massive video surveillance can be likened to Bentham's panopticon, as described by Foucault (Foucault, 1995). Because of the potential for being watched we begin to internalize the constraints of the system into our own behaviour patterns and our consciences: we in effect adopt the goals of the system.

The surveillance in new media culture goes beyond the camera. Our believed anonymity when we use the internet is a myth. Although the sheer number of users shields us from the reality, our actions do leave digital traces, in the form of 'cookies', of where we have been. The lack of privacy in email has been demonstrated in countless corporate fraud case, such as the Enron scandal. Similarly, law enforcement has been deployed regularly since 11 September 2001 in the United States and elsewhere to track various internet uses by individuals and to monitor individuals who have frequented certain sites or newslists that are deemed to represent national security or terrorist risks. The capacity to monitor is related to the ability of programs to work intelligently to find apparent risks relatively autonomously. What would appear to be an intimidating amount of information that the internet presents becomes possible to comb through with 'bots' and spiders that are very like search engines in their methods of compiling and organizing information. The memory and storage capacity of supercomputers also allows even more elaborate cross-referencing to occur even as information is simply archived.

Even that which appears benign in new media cultures can operate as a system of cybernetic control. In supermarkets in the United States patrons are given cards to access savings on their purchases. Each time you shop, you give information about your shopping preferences into an elaborate structured database. The encoding of that information determines to a degree what coupons for new products and specials are handed out, printed on the back of the receipt for the customer to use in future shopping trips. The imparting of information helps construct a consumer profile and this profile is then sold on to companies for further direct marketing and advertising. The cybernetic system in this case is wonderfully articulated to individual preferences; but it works to structure us into the larger unified objective of the consumer capitalist economy and the need to maintain the economic equilibrium through maintenance of our consumption levels and our consumption identity.

Technological adaptation

The array of products that possess interactive capabilities seems endless. The smart technology that allows for human–computer interaction where greater and greater elements of our lives are automated also patterns our thinking and our behaviour. This patterning is subtle but ever present in contemporary everyday life. What is occurring is a form of technological adaptation to the cybernetic designs of products. We become acculturated to the feedback loops and where we, as users, fit into the design of the system. The capacity to adapt to new technology is noticeably more rapid with younger people than older people. Nonetheless, we all experience a learning process with any new program, any new television guiding system or any new mobile phone system. These require us to work out the way a particular technology/system works best and coordinate our use to that objective. Over time, the processes become second nature; in other words, they become normal and relatively mundane and uneventful. For example, the process of using a mobile phone for text or sms messaging was originally onerous, yet over time heavy users have come to consider it just another form of communication – second nature.

It is important to isolate and analyse those particular moments where the technology is alien and difficult, and the process of learning the appropriate way to use it unnatural and lugubrious. Those moments point to how we are fitting into a particular cybernetic system where our interactions are still not in tune with the technology. For example, we have all experienced automated phone systems when we call large corporations or institutions. These systems have become very sophisticated. Some are organized around voice and word recognition, and respond to these by repeating key words to ensure that the program has 'understood' what the client is seeking. When automated phone systems use this technique, they are working within a range of possible responses and have determined an appropriate range. As often happens, one's particular query falls outside of the cybernetic range and presents a problem. We as users experience the frustration of interactivity that does not acknowledge our own unique cases as it attempts to group likely problems and issues. This feeling of disjuncture with a cybernetic system helps us understand the way that a particular system demands adaptation and also the way it regulates our behaviours into regularized solutions.

Inclusion/ideology

In the film *Minority Report* (2002), Tom Cruise's character is regularly hailed directly and by name by passing advertising billboards of major retailers, encouraging him to buy. The billboards determined his presence and interacted by scanning his retina and thus were able to make a vocal appeal to the character. Although the film is set in the middle of the twenty-first century, the collection of information on individuals makes this direct address through interactive advertising a distinct possibility. Through the elaborate collection of information we are included in an intricate and interconnected system of consumer culture. When we buy one product as described above, the information circulates to advertisers and producers to speculate what we might buy next. The cybernetic system then provides a series of connections that often seem endless. We receive related junk mail; we are solicited via email; we receive phone calls. Our information is bought and sold regularly in this system. The accuracy of our identity is the cybernetic component that makes these pitches increasingly more precise in their address. In a related way, digital video recorders offer a program that tries to anticipate what we would like to watch based on our past practices, and if left to its own automated controls will begin recording its selections.

How can we understand the inclusionary feeling that is produced by the interactivity of cybernetic systems that begin to read our moods and predispositions? What metaphors can be used to help us understand this contemporary structure of feeling? On one level, the system is becoming more accurate in its identification of the individual and their desires; on another we are being brought into pre-existing patterns. This represents the anxiety that besets contemporary experience. New technologies derived from the digital appear to be liberating; yet they are designs that are also highly structured.

One term derived from media and cultural studies that may have some explanatory value here is the concept of ideology. Ideology can be thought of as a useful metaphor to describe and help us move towards a useful critique of the cybernetic condition. The ruling ideas in a culture, which are typically generated by the ruling or dominant classes, defines ideology.

From a cultural studies perspective, we all live in a world of ideology; in other words, we cannot escape either its presence or its impact. Ideology positions us towards accepting the contemporary reality as legitimate, natural and normal. Like cybernetics, ideology expresses a conserving notion of what any culture (or 'system' to use cybernetic terminology) sets as its goals or objectives and thus works to pattern our behaviour. The idea of myth was originally used by Roland Barthes as a synonym for ideology and it is this use that has been advanced prominently in cultural studies as various critics have worked through the signs and sign systems of contemporary culture (Barthes, 1972). For example, the idea of the nuclear family is presented and represented in various guises in American television programmes, both dramatic and non-fictional as the norm and natural; this process of representation reinforces the myth of the family as it operates in contemporary culture. Both ideology and myth have been used as part of a structuralist understanding of our world as a cultural system. In analysing sign structures that ultimately reveal the underlying mythology of a culture, cultural studies, via structuralism and semiotics, was working towards a critique of the system that was produced.

In a similar vein, we can use this understanding of ideology from a cultural studies perspective to interpret and ultimately critique how the various strains of new media draw us into the appropriate patterns and interpretation. In cultural studies approaches, the media text 'hails' or 'interpellates' the viewer through identification. We identify with the lead character in a film or television programme, and through that process we accept to a degree that interpellation. Through that process of accepting how we have been interpellated into the meaning of the text and narrative, we are by implication brought into an acceptance of the dominant culture, its myths and ideology. In new media, with its forms of interactivity, the elaborate structures of identification are customized and highly directed through the experience of engagement in the media form. Identification is intensified to such a level that we become the player/actor in new media. For a videogame player, interpellation and identification inadequately express the level of becoming and the kinds of investment that are normal and natural. The cybernetic nature of new media, both in its potential to personalize the way that we are hailed by the various forms and the way that we are fabricated as the actors and agents in various new media texts, identifies the potential immersive power of new media to reproduce ideology and myth.

Beyond inclusion: becoming the content; becoming the object/actor

As we have already described, the capacity of new media to personalize and customize content transforms the media experience fundamentally. The interactive dimension that is at the heart of cybernetically inspired systems is all about feedback loops. The feedback loops are between machine (or its screen representations) and human actor. Feedback thus implies that the human's actions are read and interpreted, and fed back as a form of information to guide the overall objectives of the system. Through interactivity, the old division between media form and viewer is broken down more completely as the former viewer is included into the 'guidance' of the program, game or internet browser and its outcomes. This integration into the system goes well beyond the processes of identification that have helped explain the formations of pleasure we gain from watching film or television. It is more accurate to say that users of new media are becoming the content of the form. On a basic level, chat programs in their multi-logue conversations pull the user into talking for others or performing some version of the self: their correspondence in collaboration with the other members of the chatroom is the entertainment and they are performers. Similarly, webcams provide a way to become the content quite explicitly. In another vein, the avatars and skins that are employed by online gamers express their presentation of themselves and their representation among the avatars and skins of other players. In game worlds, the gamer is part of the content as well as the agent or protagonist in the game. Becoming the media image is as much part of the production by individuals of personal websites as it is an element in the transformation of television towards reality television programmes. As we shall explore in chapter six, television has made its own audience members the content of its shows in various game-like scenarios, in an effort to reproduce the 'becoming' nature and agency of new media.

Interactivity and the cybernetic commodity

One of the defining features of contemporary cultural production is that any major cultural product is released in multiple formats and variegated possible uses. Think of a Hollywood film and one thinks of a series of related products that are timed to coincide with the release of the film. Websites are not just promotional vehicles, they sometimes offer the possibility of online games. Promotional trailers envelope the film with a particular and highly constructed meaning. With action films a computer game and videogame are inevitably released. Aligned with making the film significant, television networks will broadcast a programme detailing the 'making of ...' the particular film. As the film moves through its various windows of exhibition from cinema to pay-per-view television to video rental to network television, one of the most significant of these is the DVD, which becomes a release of even further variations of the film with commentary by directors, actors and editors along with an array of interactive passages for exploration. Book releases and publications may be timed to coincide with the film's debut. Music compilations and soundtracks are timed and packaged for coordinated sale. In the case of children's films, there is massive coordination with fast-food restaurants and the marketing of character toys.

This array of related products can be thought of in cybernetic terms. The cultural product is designed to have a complete system of interaction for the audience with all forms of investment and engagement made possible and realizable. The cultural industries are coordinated to structure play in what I have called elsewhere the intertextual commodity (Marshall, 2002), but can equally be thought of as an elaborate cybernetic and relatively closed system of organizing play and engagement. The cultural product is exhausted by this array of possibilities; yet it is an intricate patterning of the audience's use so that any variation re-implicates the audience and user through the cultural commodity system. The very idea of play is commodified and structured with increasing range and variation even as the impossibility of commodifying something as rich and diverse as play seems to be more realizable in the era of interactivity and customization.

The antithesis: empowerment of the user

We have mapped the cybernetic dimensions of new media's interactivity and identified how systems and patterns serve as control mechanisms in this transformed cultural landscape; but there is always a countervailing force that envelopes cultural forms and cultural practices. In cybernetic terms it would be described as entropy – the tendency for elements to disperse and to not maintain their structure and order. From a cultural theory perspective, there is persistent evidence that the structures do not hold. Change and transformation is ever present, regularly threatening established orders and challenging the ideology that maintains the hegemony of any culture or state. Post-structuralism, which investigates the strategic and tactical dimensions that challenge structure and reshape cultural and political boundaries, can be thought of as a conceptual theory that has informed cultural studies and helps us understand how these new media systems, in their formation and use, actually produce transformed identities and subjectivities. In new media, although the patterns of how one should use these forms are highly developed in interactive and automated structures, it is equally true that these new media forms also present different possibilities that are not totally determined.

An analogy might help us understand this post-structural reality that new media forms permit: the game of chess is highly structured and patterned. Different pieces are allowed to move in specific and highly defined ways. Moreover, there are only 64 squares on a chess board and at the beginning of a game, 32 of them are occupied by different chess pieces from opposing sides. This relatively rule-based structure has led to a millennium of engagement in the complex world of chess playing. The range of positions, moves and strategies multiply exponentially in any game so that it is a nearly infinite source of variation for any player. What appears to be a highly structured game operating with many constraints has led to thousands of books advising people how to play, an elaborate international system of ranking players from expert to grand master, and endless debates among these experts about particular moves and games. This richness of variation attracted the brightest of intellects to devote their lives to chess. It was only in 1999, that a computer chess program actually beat the world chess champion for the first time.

What this analogy explains is that structures can produce endless combinations of directions that are not completely determined by the designers of new media. In fact, the new media, whether in games or websites, are specifically geared towards providing ranges of choice and direction that any player or user can take. The individual thus has to invest and commit to the process of fabricating his/her mediated experience through new media. The key difference between new and old media is the kind of subjectivity that is produced. Whereas the viewer or listener would be an adequate way of describing someone who watches television or listens to the radio, it seems inadequate to describe the dimensions of experience that are part of browsing on the web. As we have explained, interactivity engages the individual differently in the process and that difference is an endowment of a certain power in the individual.

To identify what we are calling a transformed subjectivity in new media, we need to use new terms. In film theory, the viewer defined as a film subject is 'interpellated' by the drama that is unfolding, and drawn into a form of identification with the characters. In new media such as the web, the individual is asked to choose the link and thereby be part of the process of making his media form. This may seem minor, but the changed relationship to media is very significant and has had repercussions throughout all cultural industries and into the wider dimensions of contemporary culture. This action of choosing from a menu of choices, the very tactile dimension of clicking on a mouse, shifts our default media consumption from that provided for us to one that is fabricated by us. In new media culture, we are involved in the production of the text and images that become part of our reception and pleasure. Simultaneously we are engaged in new media at the level of identification and at the level of making. Choosing what we wish to watch and read is not entirely unique to new media forms such as the web – after all, the television remote control has allowed us for many years to surf television channels with relative ease and transform television viewing practices from watching individual programmes into something that is a polyphony of messages – nevertheless new media, such as the web, have both intensified the cultural experience and made it more routine in our everyday lives. Thus, the television remote control is a precursor to the use made of the web through browsing and surfing – both cultural practices identify a productive activity that dramatically challenges conventions of production and consumption delineations that have been elemental to the experience of television.

Several metaphors could be used to describe this new subjectivity generated by new media. It is a different sensibility that acknowledges a relationship developed by the interactive functions of new media between the individual and the media form. At the beginning of this chapter I identified that the essential feature of new media is connected to the capacity of the individual to transform the media form. To uncover that relationship and to acknowledge its hybrid quality of both production and consumption, some have suggested new terms such as the 'prosumer' or the 'produser'. Certainly, other terms become more precise to identify the spectrum of involvement that is possible with new media. In distracted uses of new media, the term browser may be most accurate: an individual casually moves through screens and pages in search of articles on a particular area of interest. The subjectivity of the browser resembles how people read newspapers – they move in and out of an investment with the particular stories presented. Similarly, a browser describes a kind of use made of libraries: it is less specific and resembles the *flâneur* that Baudelaire celebrated in early twentieth-century Paris and Walter Benjamin analysed as a kind of engagement with the cityscape. Surfing has been used to describe both television watching and using the internet. Surfing implies a surface engagement with content, a distracted playfulness with what might be presented. The term also underlines the possibility of distance from material and, with that distance, anonymity. To capture the higher level of investment possible in new media forms, its subjectivity can also be identified with the idea of player. The term 'player' acknowledges an intensity of experience that envelopes the subject within the rules and dimensions of a game. In some senses, it transforms the individual into a much more circumscribed subjectivity – an identity that may be rich in detail but coordinated with the objectives of the particular game and the pleasures of the game play. Still another term, 'lurker', describes the new media experience that is most closely associated with voyeurism. Instead of participation, the subjectivity of the lurker is defined by silence in chatrooms and a desire to observe rather than engage. The lurker becomes the point where more traditional media subjectivity intersects with new media: the lurker watches and listens much as the viewer/audience subjectivity is produced by television or radio. The difference between the lurker and the viewer is the solo and individuated experiential quality of the lurker that is never part of the audience-subjectivity as it is defined by the apparatuses of television, film or radio. In this spectrum of subjectivity in new media it is important to indicate that past relationships to media can be channelled through new media. Someone working on a computer can stream audio and thereby reconstruct either recorded music or the equivalent of radio. Similarly, a film can be viewed through DVD players on the computer screen. In other words, the kinds of subjectivity that have been associated with these traditional media forms have been absorbed into the spectrum of use that defines new media. New media, as many writers have emphasized, provides for the multiplicity of engagements, sometimes simultaneously (multi-tasking) and always with the potential to be what has been described in the language of convergence as multimedia forms.

To group this spectrum of subjectivities that are part of new media can only be done accurately through thinking about what elements combine these practices. There are two central elements that help us identify the different sensibility of new media: first, the concept of the user and, second, the sensation of production in new media use.

User helps us identify the active nature of the new media subject. The individual's engagement is filled with choices and decisions. They may seem like banal decisions – for instance the decision to play a game on a mobile phone while waiting for a bus as opposed to emailing a friend – but nonetheless new media demands this kind of interaction with its user. A user then is called to interaction through the new media interface. Like the ringing or vibrating phone, new media culture's user must respond in some way or anticipate a response. The mobile phone in its collection of messages perpetually demands the user to respond to even those calls missed. Once again decisions are made and the relationship to the new media form with its capacity to interact through smart technology in its various guises maintains the connection to the user in a perpetual interaction. Similarly, browsing the internet invokes rather than evokes (Chesher, 1996) the user to advance to another link and a related web page. The modality of interaction or interactivity pulls the individual into an engagement with the website in a way that television attempts through address but never achieves because of the separation of experience. Using implies an appropriation of both the technology and its applications that can be analogous to driving a car or riding a bike. We are drawn into the various kinds of needs and responses of the particular technology and we become immersed into its needs even as we use it for our own. New media fulfils the personalization of our needs in a way that past media could never achieve. It goes beyond the dimension of choice and abundance as it has been defined by television channels and into the dimensions of interacting with personal needs and desires. New media thus provides the possibility and potential for ultimate differentiation in consumption as new media forms interact with their users. The category of the user helps us understand further the dimension of what can be a new media culture sensibility. The interconnection and convergence of technologies through new media, digitalization and convergence has allowed the channelling of greater aspects of our lives through these various technologies. There is less distinct separation of tasks, for example, between work and leisure, or between work and shopping, or even between entertainment and education.

Along with employing the concept of the user to identify the subjectivity derived from new media, this new media culture sensibility that pervades contemporary culture derives much of its cultural power and differentiation from past sensibilities, specifically through its celebration of production. New media forms increasingly naturalize both the sensation of control and the sensation of producing. In electronic games, we are invited to fabricate our identity through avatars and skins. In other words, we are incorporated into the production process of the game itself with the game's very design allowing for this integration of production. Likewise, when we use the web we are producing individuated experiences of browsing through our various choices. In fact, we are drawn to personalize our research and our discovery of information outside of its structured distribution by traditional media such as books, journals, radio and television. The proliferation of homepages on the internet designed by individuals has been exemplary of the desire to produce and how it is articulated through new media forms. What has changed is a kind of media literacy that not only leads us to interpret media, but advances us towards producing.

The user subjectivity of new media with this production ethos is a massive and unparalleled challenge to the traditions of media use that have been in place for most of the previous century. The reception/consumption ethos and dichotomy of the twentieth century has given way to a production ethos of users. In some ways, new media has heralded a transformation of contemporary culture through a democratization of cultural expression. Websites of the most personal form of production can resemble some of the most professional forms of publication. On the web, these two types of production, the professional and corporate, and the personal and idiosyncratic, now naturally intersect in a world of converged distribution and exhibition. What Hans Magnus Enzensberger had hoped for with the democratization of television production and exhibition in the early 1970s is much more realized through the web and its system of distribution (Enzensberger, 1974). Hundreds of thousands of websites appear each day that have produced a testament to the production ethos of new media subjectivity that is unparalleled in human history.

A transformed cultural politics: the politics of interactivity

What has been identified in this chapter is the new terrain of tension that has been engendered through new media. The interactive dimensions of these new forms is critical for understanding how patterns of control can be deployed; that same interactivity is the locus for new sites of creativity and productivity. As this chapter has chronicled, interactivity's parentage is the field of cybernetics. Like new media itself, cybernetics has a history connected to control and governance as well as aspects that are both encompassing and inclusive as they attempt to describe highly interconnected systems. As our various media forms have been reconstituted through their computerization and digitalization, we have to be aware of the new cultural politics that are developing.

From the negative dimension, surveillance of our activities is possible as greater aspects of our lives are channelled through computers and the internet. That potential knowledge is lurking as a form of control even as we believe in our relative anonymity online. In the United States that potential has become more real in the way that the Patriot Act 2001 has been interpreted to allow the invasion of private electronic correspondences. The divisions that once separated work from leisure are also blurring through our use of new media such as the internet both at home and in the office. Moreover, the interactive dimensions of our online experiences likewise provide 'transactional' communication about where we have been and what we have been visiting.

From the more positive dimension, the developing new media and its interactivity has transformed our status as audiences to that of participants. We have attempted to identify this shifted subjectivity with the term 'user'. The interactivity developed through a variety of software has to be seen as providing a terrain for play, which by its very definition as play has both a defined and indefinable and indeterminate status. The dimensions for that playing terrain have had wide enough parameters to lead to the proliferation of uses and activities not defined by any overarching cybernetic design that has produced the interactive interface between human and machine. This proliferation of production and activity represents the challenge of new media to contemporary culture. The engaged quality of play and activity can articulate a potential shift in politics to much more participatory designs. Likewise, new media cultures in their transformation of the audience challenges the conventions of what is seen as acceptable in cultural forms such as television and film, and moves those media to experiment with play, interactivity and participation.

Both of these dimensions, control and productive empowerment, are part of our transformed cultural politics. They embody the critical new dimensions of cultural studies in contemporary culture.

chapter three

The technological apparatus of new media cultures

Each Thursday the *New York Times* includes a section entitled 'Circuits'. 'Circuits' is devoted to new technologies generally connected to digital gadgets and new computer programs. Reviews of new pdas, discussions of digital effects in films, or new functions in the next generation of mobile phones are regular features. The critical edge is even more lightly applied than to the entertainment sections of newspapers. For eight to ten broadsheet pages, the articles express a celebration of technology and the cult of the new.

'Circuits' represents a very long tradition with relationship to technology: new inventions express the superiority of the modern over anything traditional. It is a reading of technology in a new Darwinism: each succeeding technology improves on its previous generation and liberates humanity just that much more. The *New York Times* is not alone in providing a regular space for this celebration of the future in the present manifestations of technology. Every major newspaper in the world allows for these fluff pieces about the promise of technology. In the last decade, they have developed into a larger niche of the press and have become regular features on television with whole shows such as *Tech tv* devoted to the love of new electronic and digital gadgets.

Thinking about the role of these articles helps us tackle the larger issue of technology in new media culture. These newspaper sections help create an environment of adoption of new technology. They bestow not only a building familiarity with the various gadgets' functions, but also a sense of fun and pleasure in learning and adapting to technological change. Here are a few examples of how both wonder and information are part of the introduction of new technology. In an article on satellite radio, David Pogue explains 'pay radio' via company manuals such as XM and Sirius:

> So why would people pay for radio when they have a free alternative? Because satellite radio is fantastic – a cultural source unlike any other. It's so addictive, the Sirius manual actually refers to its customers as 'users'. Because the 100 channels are largely free of commercials, their program directors don't have to appeal to all the mainstream, all the time. Satellite radio offers specialized full-time channels for pop, rock, hip-hop, dance and country... and on and on.
>
> (Pogue, 2003: E1)

The article goes on to explain how to buy a receiver and to provide more information on how it works. We are invited through the article into a world of knowing the way a technology operates but also becoming comfortable about being an early adopter of technology. Another article on the same front page guides the reader through the developments of the internet phone; but ultimately it is an article about making the leap to becoming a subscriber (Leonhardt, 2003: E1). With a picture of a computer appearing to be made out of Lincoln Logs, a popular American building toy, we discover that the encasement of a computer with its microchip boards does not have to be designed as a beige box, as manufacturers work to build a market for the 'second computer' in a household:

> For the little computer to catch on, some significant changes in the direction of computer marketing will be required – not just away from the competition for faster processing that has driven sales for years, but also toward a new design paradigm. Computers are either beige or black and businesslike, or fancied up by gaming enthusiasts with lights and pictures windows that show off the esoteric beauty of circuitry. Either way, they are mostly air; the components occupy little space inside. (Fessenden, 23 October 2003: E1, E6)

Another technology, called the Heliodisplay, is announced through a photo of the 'machine' and an accompanying text:

> Imagine a touch screen on which the elements of the image can be moved around with a fingertip. Now imagine the same scene without the screen; the image can still be moved with a fingertip, but it floats unsupported above a quietly whirring gray box that is connected to a laptop computer... The Heliodisplay's inventor, Chad Dyner, says the technology could one day replace the conventional cathode-ray tubes, liquid crystal displays and plasma screens.
>
> (Bernstein, 2003: E1)

When these various articles and images are thought of in aggregate and in conjunction with the related advertisements and commercials that circulate around new technological objects, there is something loosely coherent that emerges. Many authors have tried to describe this sensibility around technology that leads to a general embrace of its very newness. Herbert Marcuse over 40 years ago referred to this sentiment as 'technological rationality' (Marcuse, 1964). Theodor Adorno and Max Horkheimer, writing in the 1940s and coming from the same intellectual tradition, called it 'instrumental reason' (Horkheimer and Adorno, 1987). Along with Victor Ferkiss (1969) and Jacques Ellul (1964), these various critics decried how the technological society had broken down rational thought or even a clear connection to general social interest. Technology no longer served the interests of humanity, but rather we served the interests of technology and the corporations that were connected to those technologies. Part of the effect of the technologies most associated with cultural pursuits, according to Adorno and Horkheimer in particular, was an obliteration of cultivated thinking. Whether it was film or popular music, the populace was blinded by the sheer sensation and drawn in by the banality of the entertainment to not see their true interests (1987: 121–69).

Many of these serious debates about technology flourished in the middle of the twentieth century in the era of film, television and radio. Their critiques, like those of Lewis Mumford, were often directed towards some sort of homeostasis and extended well beyond the cultural into the deleterious effects of the technology on the environment (Mumford, 1934). With the development of digital culture expressed by the ubiquitous placement of the microchip and computer hardware and software across an array of products, forms and practices, can these same arguments be made or has the digital reconstruction of our world pushed us to new considerations and new directions for our critical inquiry?

Some more recent writing on digital culture has at least tried to answer that question. For instance, Levinson and many others have been drawn to Marshall McLuhan's reading of media to understand digital culture (Levinson, 1999). McLuhan's thinking on media and technology tended to be descriptive as opposed to critical; but his insights were manifold. McLuhan thought of technology as an extension of our senses. Moreover, he saw emerging with electronic technology the capacity to connect intelligence or the actual outering of the nervous system into an elaborate network (McLuhan, 1965). Some of these ideas actually make more sense when they are linked to new media technology than they do to any of the technologies contemporaneous with McLuhan between the 1950s and 1970s. In adapting that thinking to contemporary media technology, McLuhan's terminology of hot and cool media has some value. Hot media meant that they were overly defined and complete. Film and print tended to be hot media. Cool media were those that allowed for greater interaction, where the audience as participants completed the form and its meaning. Although it is still hard to fully appreciate the 'cool' qualities of television, McLuhan's insights make sense when we think of technologies such as games or browsing the web (Burnett and Marshall, 2003). In these new media forms we can see that the user completed what is presented for him either through playing the game or constructing the web search.

McLuhan's other insight of relevance was that it is more significant to think of the medium than its content – in a procession of succession, the content of the current media form was that of the previous form. Film's content was derived from its predecessors – the novel and the play; television's content tended to be derived from film and radio. From McLuhan's perspective, if we concentrate on what the medium does we can extrapolate its future in terms of its uses and how it transforms the social world (McLuhan, 1965). Thus with new media such as electronic games or the internet, we can begin thinking about how the actual form begins to shape us individually and socially. Bolter and Grusin more recently theorized how new technologies remediated older forms, and have produced a slightly more nuanced reading of technology and cultural form than McLuhan. (Bolter and Grusin, 2000).

Because of the simple relationship between technology and its capacity to transform society, McLuhan is rightly labelled a technological determinist. Technological determinism has two principal weaknesses as a way to conceptualize any technology's role in a culture. First of all, in McLuhan's case, it sets up the communication form as all powerful in its capacity to transform the social world. Like his precursor, Harold Adams Innis, who wrote about the rise and fall of empires within the context of dominant technologies of communication (Innis, 1950, 1951), McLuhan places too much importance on one factor in shaping the society. Second, and this is related to the first weakness, McLuhan's overemphasis on the medium allows him to overlook political and economic forces that have allowed the emergence for particular ends of specific media technologies. His approach simplifies the way that technology emerges as well as how it is deployed for certain ends.

The most interesting transformation of McLuhan's thinking in the late twentieth-century can be seen in the work of Jean Baudrillard. Where McLuhan presented an epiphanic vision of the future through electronic technology (Kroker, 1986), Baudrillard from the same vantage point underlines the dangers of this technologically simulated world. Baudrillard's concept of the simulacrum is a study of the implications of the media form, where reality is replaced by an elaborate construction of reality that he labels hyper-reality (Baudrillard, 1983). References in hyper-reality no longer refer to the real but the fabricated surface that has been produced by technologies such as television. Wars such as the first Gulf War are replaced by its representation and ultimately its simulation through the televisual (Baudrillard, 1991).

Although there is merit and useful insight in Baudrillard's work, its claims like McLuhan's are driven to an extreme conceptualization of the social world. Baudrillard's writing itself migrates for effect to hyperbole, and overstates the power of the simulacrum and its self-referential constitution of the hyper-real. With some success, Baudrillard's approach does integrate a kind of political economy behind the development of the simulacrum and this way his work betters that of McLuhan; nonetheless, his approach does not capture the experiential quality of the lived cultural condition of new media.

For some writers who have studied the social implications of digital technology, new media cultures have been linked to the postmodern moment. Sherry Turkle's work on internet and game lives, *Life on the Screen* (1995), begins to delineate the fractured identity that is part of new media. People take on multiple identities and are comfortable with this less coherent conception of the self. Turkle's reading of this state is to connect it to the dispersed identity that is at the heart of postmodernism. The postmodern condition, from Lyotard's position, is represented by a number of elements, with perhaps the most important being that it is a tactical response to the failure of modernity. The postmodern moment is temporally located with the decline in the work of the great meta-narratives that have held societies together (Lyotard, 1985): for example, the decline of religion, the decline of the purity of Marxism as an answer to capitalism, the dissipation of coherent gender roles and identity, the uncertainty in the belief in both technology and progress, and the dispersion of clear national identities in the transnational multicultural migration.

Writers such as Donna Haraway have made the link much more transparent among technology, postmodernism and the transformation of the self. In her cyborg manifesto, Haraway identifies how the integration of technology with the human has allowed for women to break free from their structured gendered identities into different possible non-binary conceptualizations of the self (Haraway, 1991). N. Katherine Hayles, via science-fiction literature and science, also investigates the slippages between the human and the machine as technology begins to represent and integrate with the human (Hayles, 1999).

What becomes evident from reading these writers that have linked technology to the postmodern condition is that they have identified a certain sensibility that is part of new media and the cultures it has spawned. It is important then to understand that there are linkages between the constant presence of digital technology and how we conduct ourselves in the world. To comprehend this sensibility, it is useful to draw on a metaphor that was developed in film analysis in the 1960s and 1970s. Christian Metz attempted to express the process of engagement that film viewing entailed (Metz, 1982). He wanted to capture that cinema was more than a technology in that it produced an effect that paralleled the dream state. To encompass this complex constitution of a certain subjective experience by the viewer he used the term 'cinematic apparatus'. The apparatus produced a subjectivity that placed the viewer into a psychological state where one could analyse the compelling quality of images. The apparatus was a combination of the machines of exhibition, the physical location of watching the film in a darkened hall with the 'fourth wall' illuminated and the entire process that went into producing this dream state.

The concept of apparatus adapted from cinema studies can be used to explain the transformed relationship digital technology and new media have produced in contemporary culture. This technological apparatus produces a new relationship to the world; this idea parallels the work of Turkle and Hayles in its expression of a shifted cyber-generated identity. In less dramatic ways, the technological apparatus sets up a digital sensorium that ultimately operates in its normalcy as a loose ideology within the culture. The newspaper articles discussed at the beginning of this chapter are part of the support structure for naturalizing our relationship to new media and new technology. To use the idea of the apparatus is to implicate not only the technology but its effect on people. What emerges from the uses of the various technologies – the internet, mobile phones with instant messaging and the capacity to take digital photos, electronic games and their forms of interactivity, smart technology in home appliances, GPS guidance systems in cars, portable digital calendars and notebooks, digital books, DVDs, digital cameras, MP3 players and so on – is that we implicitly understand that these apparently diverse technologies with divergent functions are all very much related. The regularity of the use of the digital machines is that we have naturalized the expansive presence of the digital and the microchip in the way that we move through the world. The kinds of interaction that digital technology produces become second nature to our being and normalize ideal forms of interaction. Like the cinematic apparatus, the technological apparatus surrounds, mediates and becomes part of our identity and relationship to the world. The digital world produces us as technological subjects.

The technological apparatus has many components that produce this complex web, which both visibly and invisibly work in contemporary culture. It should be understood that the apparatus has economic and political dimensions that are often overlooked because of the power of its ideology of technology. From a cultural studies perspective, our analysis of the technological apparatus is a study of access and exclusion. The questions that need to be asked about new media culture revolve around the possibilities and the constraints of the current technological apparatus.

Networked world and the digital divide

In late November 1999, the World Trade Organization (WTO) met in Seattle. Rather than another trade meeting with dignitaries and debates about working on the inclusion of China as a member, the Seattle meeting became known for the strength and breadth of a protest.

Thousands of people connected to unions, student groups and environmental organizations, and other social activists from local, national and international origins came to voice their opposition to the development of international trade. The level of organization and coherence of the protestors' message was such a surprise to the news media that it became a major media event. Groups not normally associated with each other bonded in a grander anti-globalization movement. In fact, many writers proclaimed that this was the beginning of the movement as a unified front opposing trade liberalization.

There are many elements of this protest that are remarkable, but two directly exemplify contrasting dimensions of new media cultures. First of all, the level of organization depended on a very sophisticated network that fundamentally stemmed from the internet. Group lists and listservs connected various parties, internationally, in discussion. Debates and arguments could develop into political strategies through this online world. The boundaries of the internet and the World Wide Web were not constrained by national borders or specific types of work or activity. What had developed online was a commonality of interest and realization that the low wages of one part of the world directly affected another part of the world. Not since the trades union movement of the 1930s had such a unified front been presented. The movement depended on the accessibility of the technology to facilitate its cross-institutional discussions. As much as the cables and wires of the internet are networks of networks, the anti-globalization movement similarly became a network of networks that criss-crossed internationally and domestically via the internet. The kinds of connection possible, whether they were through university networks, library networks or personal internet connections in the home, created a different politics of possibility that are fundamentally different than that imaginable prior to 1990.

What the internet provided was an apparatus to expand discussion along new pathways. To understand this further, it is useful to think of Deleuze and Guattari's concept of the rhizome and the machinic assemblage (Deleuze and Guattari, 1987). A distinctively different organization of meaning developing not through something that is hierarchical, but rather in expansive web-like extensions and reverberations, appears to be accompanying our technological apparatus, which is what Deleuze and Guattari describe as a 'machinic assemblage'. Like the technological apparatus, the assemblage is not completely determined as to its directions and objectives. It functions to pull together multiple points into moments of connected structure and coherence that can disperse as quickly as they congealed. The assemblage facilitated through the internet allowed for the development of the Seattle moment and the periodic reappearance of this politics at other international trade meetings that have occurred in Quebec, Genoa, Melbourne and Washington over the last half-decade. The technology itself – in this case the new media form of the internet – has no central control or general that determines its uses. It can permit the temporary development of new clusters of related interests that surface in political protest at some future event. Thus, what we observe in contemporary new media cultures is the operation of rhizomes along surfaces rather than roots. This surface movement and linkage presents a different form of cultural production than that, for example, formerly organized around the nation and nationalism. Thus, Seattle's protest politics was actually a different kind of opposition; farmers from South America were now linked to workers from the fading industrial heartlands of the United States.

Along with new network formations, the Seattle anti-globalization movement represents a new reality of access. The wired world has permitted a wide range of people access to the internet. It has produced a heightened level of communication that has allowed a loose network to move from some virtual status of shared political sentiments to an organizational presence on the streets of Seattle among other key cities. This kind of exchange at one time would have depended on governmental cooperation and organization as well as deep resources to maintain contact. What has developed in the last 15 years is the capacity of larger numbers of the population to communicate relatively cheaply via email to individuals and groups in other parts of the world. The instantaneous speed of this communication makes the network possible and real. Paradoxically, if one considers the internet a key technology of globalization, it is also a key technology of anti-globalization. As Manuel Castells has documented in his three-volume *Network Society*, even regional politics has been transformed by new networking politics. The Zapatista Amerindians of Mexico have successfully mobilized their resources of resistance to the demands of the central Mexican government partly through local and international connections via the internet (Castells, 1997: 68–83; see also Kowal, 2002).

The second element that the Seattle protest exemplifies about new media cultures can also be understood as an access issue. Not all of the planet has access to these information flows and networks that have become second nature to many individuals. The technological apparatus thus must be seen as modalized around exclusion as much as access and inclusion. Some have labelled this difference in relation to new media technologies the 'digital divide'. Others, such as Kroker, refer to a new class – datatrash – made up of the discarded groups in any culture who are not connected to the new structures and machines of information. (Kroker, 1994). About 450 million people currently use the internet (Nielsen/Netratings, 2004). Internet hosts exceed 100 million. Despite this gigantic network, with the world population approaching 6 billion this large number of internet users is still less than 10 per cent of the world's population. Indeed, even telephone access is unheard of in many parts of some African countries. The reality is that new media is a technological sensibility of the most affluent areas of the world. It can divide populations completely. For example, in India, Bangalore with its massive software industry is very much part of new media culture for those working in the industry; but there are large segments of Bangalore itself and India more widely where this relationship to newer media such as the web and the internet is nonsensical. The globalization that new media represents also excludes from participation large sectors of the contemporary world. There is a banding of the middle classes in many countries that begins to resemble their counterparts in other parts of the world. The experience of new media culture in the way that we have described it is fundamentally banded and branded with this socio-economic divide.

The political-economic dimension of the technological apparatus of new media

Beyond the insights that the 1999 Seattle protest has helped explain about the technological apparatus, it is important to go further into the political and economic underpinnings of new media culture. Much like their predecessors, the new technologies have conflicting origins and compromised ideals. Certainly, as the Seattle example has revealed, there are quasi-public elements to the emergence of new media culture. Internet use can be likened to the emergence of the public utilities of electricity and to a lesser extent the telephone service, at least in more affluent nations. Under Al Gore's National Information Infrastructure (NII), US government policy was working towards ensuring access to the internet. Schools and public libraries were wired so that the World Wide Web could be made available broadly. In fact, the infrastructure of networking computers was originally subsidized by the Pentagon in the United States via the Department of Defence's Advanced Research Projects Agency (DARPA). Similar government initiatives were developed in most western countries. Some nations saw the information technologies as a springboard to new international status as part of the economic elite; Malaysia, for example, wired an 'information corridor' outside of Kuala Lumpur, its capital. Australia's desire to become the 'Creative Nation' in the mid-1990s was likewise focused on connecting to the information-rich side of the digital divide. Singapore became the most wired city (and state) on the planet, and modelled this expansion to ensure its economic present and future. Korea has worked to expand wireless and wired coverage to both domestic and business sites in order to become one of the most 'connected' nations in the world.

The objective of governments in building infrastructure and thereby providing access to their people was not, however, entirely modalized around simple and utopian ideals of public good. The emergence of new media cultures has been in an era of what is variously described as economic rationalism or neoliberalism around trade. Some of the key industry sectors of public policy and control have been deregulated – the airline industry, public utilities and broadcasting are just three examples – as governments have allowed 'market' forces and the economy to determine costs and have given up their long-held role of protecting the public interest. States have sold off their government-owned industries in some cases and outsourced their contracts for other government programmes as the number of public service government employees has declined. With these various forms of deregulation, corporations have gained unprecedented power. The worldwide decline in trades unions is also an emblem of economic rationalism. Collective action as represented by public policy or the actions of trades unions has been supplanted by a more expansive ideal of individual representation of interests.

Out of these developments a certain schizophrenia in government action has emerged. On the one hand, incredible liberalization has occurred. Corporations and capital are much more liquid and movable than ever before. A factory can be relocated rapidly to another city or country where its directors deem that the cost of labour is significantly cheaper. Indeed, the emergence of Bangalore over the last 15 years as a software capital for the computer and information industries was motivated precisely by the presence of a large, cheap but well-educated workforce. The flight of manufacturing to China in the last half-decade is similarly motivated by corporations looking for cheap labour. On the other hand, governments have been instrumental in setting up the infrastructure for this mobility of capital. The global internet, along with various business intranets that connect to corporations, has been heavily subsidized by governments. Along with many other dividends to society, this government subsidization has facilitated corporations to control their multinational empires from a distance. Information networks permit head offices to be in New York, London or Redmond, while the manufacturing, or possibly the software coding, is completed elsewhere. Connectivity to these information networks is critical, then, for the movement of capital and for a very transformed international order.

In many ways, the 1990s represented the first generation of this new economy. Corporations such as Nike could have their design centres in North America along with their corporate headquarters and have the actual manufacturing of their shoes carried out in Thailand (Klein, 2000). In this way, intellectual labour was spatially divided from material or physical labour in a manner unprecedented in history. The location of the more industrial and potentially environmentally dangerous elements of contemporary new media production would often be located in the poorer and least environmentally regulated countries, while the work carried out in North America and Europe would be apparently clean in its completion, via silence and the electronic hum of computers and networks. The economic boom in the United States and western Europe was fundamentally built on this divide and transformation of industries: cheaper labour in another part of the world and new kinds of efficiencies achieved through information technologies in the first world.

The second generation of the new economy is now taking hold. Instead of the mobility of only manufacturing, there is now a movement of the information and creative industry sectors to other parts of the world. If graphic designers are cheaper in Romania than they are in New York, then those elements of production can be, and are, done in such a new location. The film industry has been on the cutting edge of this form of production, which is now becoming standard in other industries. For example, the digital effects for a film can be produced in Brisbane and downloaded for post-production editing in London, while the musical score is developed in Hollywood. The assemblage of a major motion picture is now often very international. The actual shooting of the film is no longer necessarily set in the city where the story is supposed to take place. Toronto, with its cheaper dollar but trained film crews, has become the location for many films 'set' in New York, Chicago or Philadelphia. The most notorious of these relocations was the film *Chicago*, which was actually filmed in Toronto.

The new economy's second generation is expanding and proliferating in many different directions. Johnson & Johnson, an American household goods manufacturer, now has its company benefits support services operating in India for its American workers (*New York Times*, 8 December 2003). Many banks, cable companies and internet service providers divide up the duties of their various financial services across countries and occasionally internationally. Part of the second generation of the new economy is the extension of the virtual quality of the workplace, its very location is no longer a material entity. Regions become known as telecommunication call centres for companies. For example, in Canada, two of the poorer provinces, New Brunswick and Newfoundland, have developed new specialities as the telephone service contact home of major corporations.

The repercussions of the second generation are only now being felt. At present, there is a migration of information-related positions out of the most affluent countries to places such as Bangalore. The second generation identifies the extension of the liquidity of capital so that intellectual labour derived from the manipulation of information is no longer attached to the first world. It is a sign that as long as there is sufficient educational development in any particular location, it can become a new hub of the information economy. If the cost of production can be reduced by the migration and the quality of the workforce can be maintained, new 'design' elements of production will be vulnerable to relocation. The major beneficiaries of the second generation are those countries that have built a higher-education infrastructure that can rival that of Europe or North America. India and China have at least that capability for a fraction of their populations as they emerge as regions of expansion of this new generation of informational capitalism.

The transformation of work ... and play

Along with its migration transnationally, the nature of work is changing in new media culture. As we have already discussed, the first generation of the new media economy led to the flight of more manual labour to the so-called third world while its information design and its financing remained in the more affluent countries. Elements of this kind of labour replicate the poor working conditions during the industrialization of the UK and other parts of Europe and North America in the nineteenth century. In the United States, a cheap labouring class was drawn from successive waves of new immigrants. In Europe, it was drawn from the displaced farm workers who migrated to become the new urban working class. In the contemporary factory, there may be elements of assembly-line production of goods that have been automated; nonetheless the conditions of work and the compensation in these new factories are challenging and often exploitative.

The more 'intellectual' forms of labour have also been transformed. One of the central changes has been the rapid decline in long-term employment for the information classes. Once again, the film industry has served as a herald for many other related sectors. Work, particularly in the information and technology sectors, has become much more project-orientated. The mid-twentieth-century model of employment in the computer industry was that of IBM. Workers could guarantee lifetime employment with the same corporation. Similar models of lifetime employment were part of the post-Second World War economy in Japan. The 1990s brought to the fore shorter contracts and the desire for corporations to have flexibility in their workforces. When a particular software was completed or a complete game had gone retail, the new media company would downsize, and then rehire when a new project or contract was established. Compensation, particularly in the 1990s, for many start-up new media companies was often divided between salary and a vested interest in the company itself through stock options. Loyalty to a company was no longer built through continuity, but through this stake in the company's fortunes. The attitude of these new media employees has also changed. Success is determined not by longevity of employment in a particular corporation and internal advancement, but rather by building a portfolio of interesting projects and increasing responsibility for the completion of each successive project. This attitude of shifting from company to company and project to project was very possible in the economic boom of the 1990s, but as the international economy and in particular the new media industry 'consolidated' and hired less in the early twenty-first century, the itinerant project worker could often have long periods of unemployment. The surplus of new media labour now benefits the new media corporations specifically because of the new standard in the industry of project-orientated work.

Twinned with the expansion of project-orientated work, were many physical changes to the work environment. In the industries of new media, from start-up internet companies such as Yahoo! and software game manufacturers such as Electronic Arts, to digital film companies such as Pixar and the software giant Microsoft, workplaces were designed for long hours with spaces to play along with cubicles for work. Creative work environments may include game spaces where workers can play table tennis, pool or computer games. Former factory spaces became attractive for start-up companies to develop large and expansive open-office designs. With much software and game coding demanding collaborative work, team workplaces came into vogue. Unorthodox work habits were also encouraged, particularly in the 1990s. Working through the night was facilitated by ensuring that the workplace had couches and beds for naps. Because work was based on projects and their completion, in some new media companies encouraging workers to virtually live at work in order to focus on the project was increasingly commonplace. The separation of work and non-work in new media for many employees became harder to discern. As some writers have pointed out, the new workplace was modelled on American university residence or dormitory life for engineers and computer science majors. Studying for exams or completing a project for their subjects was replicated by the deadlines and workloads of the new media corporation. The 'fun' environment of the dorm was reproduced in the cooperative and team bonding space of the workplace.

The technologies of new media have also transformed the relationship to employment in many other settings and industries that are perhaps less spectacular than the work and play environment of new media companies. The historical penetration of mobile phones presents an interesting reading of how new technologies develop first as business tools and then become equally significant in the maintenance of social and family networks and other non-work activities. In the 1980s, the mobile phone was associated with the car phone of the busy executive. The size of the phone limited its early portability. Nonetheless, the mobile phone became a standard business accessory by the early 1990s in many affluent countries. Companies such as Nokia and Ericsson became world leaders in the manufacture of mobile phones partly through promoting their various uses. For those running a small business, the phone allowed them to have a virtual office while on the road to new clients. Similar uses of being on the job site but still in contact with the office enhanced the value of the mobile phone for trades people. Increasingly, by the late 1990s, as the business market was saturated and offered little room for further growth, advertisements for mobile phones became much more focused on their capacity to help families stay in touch. Service providers began offering plans that permitted 'unlimited weekend minutes' or late-evening discounts, which led to the mobile phone's further infiltration into everyday life. Multiphone packages were offered to families. Other advertisements emphasized the safety and security value of the phone and played on 'what if' scenarios: what if your car broke down late at night in a dangerous part of the city or on a remote stretch of motorway?

Over the first half-decade of the twenty-first century, the mobile phone has become ubiquitous. In certain countries, the number of mobile phones now exceeds the number of landlines. As the market for phones has moved to a younger demographic of teens and pre-teens, phones have been sold on more surface differences. Different covers can 'personalize' a phone as a style accessory. Text messaging capabilities, screen qualities and the increasing number of games available have become some of the selling features of contemporary phones. Ringtones, digital camera add-ons, web and email capabilities have made the mobile phone more useful for business, but ultimately a technology that has crossed from being one designed for work to one of play and connection.

The desktop computer has had a similar trajectory as a business technology. Office computers, used most prevalently for word processing and accounting spreadsheets, have been bundled with simple games for more than 15 years. Once office computers were networked externally they became technologies of both work and non-work. Web surfing, internet chat and email expanded the work components into other needs and desires by workers. The blending of work and personal pursuits has allowed the desktop computer to facilitate what de Certeau describes as tactical moments of resistance at work away from the directives of the employer (de Certeau, 1984). Screen savers have developed to 'cover the tracks' of errant office workers. With a simple toggle, they can move from what they were pursuing to an image of a spreadsheet before any superior can catch them. A recent commercial on e-trading on the stock exchange presented a similar scenario: workers pursuing their own objectives by trading online before the boss could see that they weren't working on their designated tasks. Research tools such as Nielsen's Mediametrix have been charting the use of the internet in the workplace and differentiating it from home use. What is clear in longitudinal studies of the sites visited most frequently during work hours is the popularity of non-work-related sites as employees use their work time for more personal pleasures and pursuits (Neilsen Netratings, 2004).

The opening up of the home market for the personal computer has always been similarly twinned: the home computer was designed to expand work and productivity into the home while it offered the possibility of and potential for fun and pleasure. The more mundane tasks of keeping records and files have expanded as computers have become a resource for the downloading of music, storing and collecting images and photos, and playing computer games. For children, the home computer matched this business and pleasure divide. Ostensibly purchased and networked to the web for homework, study and writing papers, the computer was also a site for play and fun. Indeed, educational software has often been designed to blend play with learning by embedding the pedagogical objectives into a computer game. This insight has been heavily invested in by the US Army in helping train its soldiers via computer games to produce the simulation of combat encounters.

In general, new media culture has made work ubiquitous and possible in any and every location imaginable for information workers. Non-work time, whether evenings or vacations, has been colonized by the possibility and potential of work by the technology of portability and the accessibility of replicating a work environment in a variety of settings even beyond the home. But work now is not so simply constituted because the technologies have opened up the dimension of play as an ever present possibility. Games are as conspicuous in their ready availability in all environments. What new media cultures have produced is a new sensibility that sometimes incorporates, sometimes resists, but always acknowledges play in the new economy of work.

Conclusion: identity play inside the technological apparatus of new media

This chapter has identified the implications of the technology of new media in contemporary culture. Principally, the elaborate and pervasive technological apparatus that digitalization has spawned has led to a shifted subjectivity. It has altered the patterns of connection in societies, it has led to new constellations of economic power, and it has transformed the relationship between work, leisure, place and space in dramatic ways.

It would be an oversimplification to say that the technology produced these changes. There are economic motivations and formations of cultural power that are part of the development and adoption of any new technology. Through understanding the entire complex social context within which technologies arise, we can discern how new technologies become integrated into the cultural milieu to become second nature to their users. The status of second nature, where the given technology is incorporated into everyday lives, is what we mean by the technological apparatus. The technological apparatus produces a sensibility around the new sensorium of digital machines that service us, extend our vision, interact with us, inform us and provide us with transformed notions of play and pleasure.

The technological apparatus detailed here does not apply universally and consistently. There are generational, educational, economic, gender and regional differentiations in the power of the apparatus to produce this new sensibility. We can readily see these divides when we observe the different speed at which a 10 year old acquires new computer skills in comparison to a 65 year old. Where new media forms such as the computer are second nature and have always been in existence for the 10 year old, the 65 year old has different relationships to technology and the computer itself, serving to mystify its functions somewhat.

To summarize the implications of the technological apparatus, it is useful to look at the various divides that have been produced more directly. New media cultures produce different kinds of contested terrains where distinctive cultural struggles are coming to the fore. The following sections describe some of the key dichotomies that have been developing both within the logic of the technological apparatus and outside of its ideological range.

Access/exclusion

The digital divide comes in many forms and permutations. Within cultures, gender, generation and relative affluence divide the uses made of particular kinds of technologies. Between nations, transnational corporations and the organization of the new economy has worked to set up new divides. Governments have straddled the fence in terms of opening up access for their populations to use new technology, while simultaneously supporting the development of international trade that is designed to produce further divides and forms of exclusion. A new form of politics has emerged from the expansion of new media technology. One the one hand, there are the international trade organizations and the major economic powers who support trade liberalization and espouse the positive benefits of globalization; on the other hand, there has emerged a large, heterogeneous yet united anti-globalization movement that has been assisted in its organization by the internet. The debates that emerge and resonate from this clash are principally about the aspirations of access and the repercussions of exclusion.

On a different plane of experience within new media culture, access is primarily about democratizing a particular technology. Software can be made accessible and easy to operate – and this has been its progression over the last 20 years. Computers demand less technical knowledge as the techniques of interaction are made more intuitive and seamless between human and machine. This kind of accessibility is qualitatively different than access to older media such as television broadcasts. What new media culture's access implies is the ability to engage, transform and manipulate in some way what is produced by the technology. Exclusion from these new cultural practices of engagement and interaction of any cultural form risks its future marginalization.

Personalization/collectivity

Within the technological apparatus of contemporary culture, new media continues a trajectory that has been advancing for more than 40 years. Since the portable transistor radio, the movement towards the personalization of media has continued and accelerated. It is partly an economic imperative: as markets saturate, new markets need to be generated. Multiple television sets in households with distinctive uses, clock radios in each bedroom and the Sony Walkman are all examples of the expansion of media for more personalized use that were well in place more than 20 years ago. All these developments assisted the electronic hardware manufacturers; all are historical markers of the expansion of the personalization of media in affluent countries. New media forms have built on this sensibility of personal forms further. Computers are designed generally for one user. Notebook computers further personalize the activity of computer use. Videogames moved from publicly accessible arcades to home televisions to hand-held 'game boys'. The telephone transmogrified into a personal machine that is literally carried everywhere by the individual. MP3 players and iPods provide an elaborate, personalized collection of musical preferences that can be programmed to individual moods. The personalization of media has become a conspicuous form of consumption that sometimes becomes divorced from the technology's irregular use. Nonetheless, the sensibility in new media cultures is very much towards personalized media.

In contrast, the technological apparatus has produced astounding possibilities of connection between people that break down the apparent isolation of experience produced by personalized media. It would be an interesting study to compare the frequency of phone use by those who own a mobile phone with that of those who do not. The perpetual reality of connection to someone else moments after thinking of the person has without doubt produced many calls between individuals. This potential of connection as a sensibility of new media cultures is further underlined through the use of the internet, short text messaging, emails, internet relay chat programs and the rapidly expanding internet telephone services. Even traditional telephone services have declined in cost for long-distance and international calls. New media cultures are connected cultures.

The result of this new level of connectivity is new formations of collectivity. The anti-globalization movement represents one cluster that has led to coordinated, direct political activism. Interest groups can now connect and meet virtually much more easily. Although it is in its nascent form, a new kind of populist politics is emerging that is very dependent on new media forms such as the internet. Howard Dean's Democratic presidential candidacy in 2003 and 2004 (which is investigated further in the next chapter), and to a lesser degree Arnold Schwarzenegger's successful campaign to become California's governor in 2003, represented a different connection between the political process and the populace. New 'public spheres' are emerging as dialogue and conversation are occurring online and having impacts politically. In a similar vein, new collectivities or virtual communities are coalescing around their own specific interests, which are not producing the same public culture that was filtered through the mediation of newspaper coverage, radio and television through most of the latter half of the twentieth century. The phenomenon of music file sharing, which is explored further in chapter four, is also indicative of new kinds of communities and connections that are challenging many formerly stable dimensions of contemporary culture.

Work/play

As detailed in this chapter, the nature of work is in state of flux. Its location, the organization of working hours, and the limited contracts designed around projects indicate that work is not thought of in the same way as it was in the middle of the twentieth century. In many ways, there is a decline in organizational commitment, and the bureaucratically driven organizational man of middle management is disappearing as an entity. New kinds of position have developed, with the emergence particularly in the informational and digital industries of a workforce that is incredibly mobile and more driven by a kind of personal entrepreneurship. Education has become pivotal in this transformation in work as jobs are dependent on knowledge of programming and engineering in new media culture.

Play has traditionally been the province of children. In new media cultures, play has moved centre-stage in its significance in the creative forms of production and recreation. As detailed in chapter five on game culture, play is now organizing the entertainment industry beyond its formerly limited repertoire in toys and board games. Play has become the driving creative force in the film industry as much as in the organization of work and creativity in the software and internet work environment. In some ways, play has been colonized in the era of new media cultures to expand the impact and investment by users in the new technologies. Technophilia, the sheer love of technology, is behind the embrace of gadgets that are simultaneously games and business machines. Mobile phones and palm pilots lead the way in blending work needs with those of play and recreation.

Production/reception

As much as the technological apparatus of new media cultures resembles the operation of the cinematic apparatus, there are qualitative differences in experience that identify a clear shift in subjectivity. As emphasized in chapter two, new media via interactivity has allowed for the development of a different relationship to the cultural form. With the cinematic apparatus producing a cultural imaginary in the viewer that moves between the text and forms of identification, the technological apparatus of new media has led to a much more producer-like subjectivity in contemporary culture. Reception, which is central to the experience of film, in new media cultures is only an element that ultimately leads the user or viewer towards self-production. This new focus on production manifests itself across new media that we shall explore in the coming chapters: the making of websites, the participation in electronic games, the involvement in lifestyle and reality television, the home use of digital video and still cameras, and the digital manipulation and/or downloading of music are some of the most prominent examples that identify the producerly subjectivity fostered by new media. From an industry vantage point, the production aspect of new media becomes a site for the expansion of markets. Instead of selling television programmes and advertisements, new media sells software for the making of video and images. Production by the user becomes a new level of consumption. Something akin to craft and craft knowledge is part of this drive to make and produce. Simplifying the technology of production – that is, developing software that is understandable – widens the dimensions of production to the amateur aficionado and expands the market for the technologies of production.

As much as we have identified the conceptual differences of new media and the cultural practices they have propagated in the first three chapters of this book, we need to go further in analysing the particularities of this transformation. Each of the remaining four chapters works in detail through specific cultural forms – the internet, electronic games, digital television and film – and examines how they articulate this new sensibility and subjectivity for the user with regard to their role in generating distinctive new media cultures.

chapter four

The internet: the multimedia-accessible universe and the user

More than any other new media technology, the internet has represented the idea of change and newness within contemporary culture. A whole new vernacular has developed from its myriad forms that underline its pervasive influence and its normalization in our lives. The idea of a computer virus has taken on equivalent status to a flu epidemic in terms of warnings, types of inoculation and preventative care and the dire consequences of infection. Spam, formerly a luncheon meat, is now understood as junk email. Brand names such as eBay or Amazon, which were non-existent in the early 1990s, now represent types of buying and selling via the World Wide Web engaged in by millions. Perhaps the most interesting neologism to emerge from the web in the last five years is the verb 'to google'. Google, the most popular of search engines to tour the vast terrain of the web, has become a shorthand abbreviation for doing a web search for some particular fact. People 'google' other people to find out how they are represented via the web in a new variation on the game of six degrees of separation.

Despite this familiarization with the various practices that have developed through the internet, as a cultural form it is difficult to analyse because of its ubiquity. As touched on in chapter one, the internet has effectively remediated many forms of communication under its rather large umbrella of activities. Although letter-writing has continued, email has to be seen as replacing some of that practice and has sped up its delivery. Instant messaging, with its whole range of communication abbreviations and emoticons, represents something between real-time dialogue, conversation through text and something approaching telephone conversations. Many web pages are designed in the tradition of magazines. Others, such as atomfilms.com, provide the opportunity to screen short films. Still others are designed to showcase musical talent or the latest sports results via audio or video files or both. Layered over many of these sites are pop-up advertisements. Indeed, even simple internet games involve multi-tasking: while playing, one is usually invited to engage in chat with one's opponent.

As opposed to being a simple media form, the internet represents the tendency that we see in many new media: it is a multimedia form. Because of this quality, the internet also embodies the cultural and an industry imaginary around a converged media form. In previous eras of media use, the isolation of particular functions produced the cultural form and ultimately the cultural practice. Thus a phone, in its simplicity of emphasizing networking oral communication over distance, achieved pre-eminence. Still cameras were designed exclusively for the reproduction of the image as photograph. To a degree, technologies such as television and film are combinatory in their capacities through their matching of elaborate and multilayered soundtracks with moving images, and thus represent the origins of multimedia. What distinguishes the internet from these quite elaborate precursors are two fundamentally different technological structures.

First, as its name suggests, the internet is more than anything else a network of networks interlaced and augmented via the intricate network of telephone cables and more recently cable television lines. Much like the phone system, the internet is a carrier of content, but does not determine the nature of that content. Attempts to regulate internet content by various government organizations from Singapore and Australia to the overturned American Communication Decency Act 1996, have struggled precisely because it is simply a network of connections and nothing more.

Second, the internet can handle the movement of massive amounts of information in many different directions simultaneously through packet switching. Packet switching was originally developed to maximize the use of the old supercomputers through timesharing: because the computing time of any given user's job would be relatively minor for these mainframes, it was possible for people to feel as if they were all working at the same time at their respective connected terminals while only paying for seconds of computation (Gere, 2002: 67–8). Similarly, it is possible for many people to be on the same website at the same time. Information is bundled in smaller digitally structured packets that are reassembled on each computer into the text, images and graphics in pieces that download. This means that there is a sharing of the lines: as one packet is downloading on to a given computer, another packet is uploading. The effect of this movement and use of the network is that, in some forms, such as the World Wide Web, the internet begins to resemble a broadcasting entity. In its other forms, it can produce real-time chat.

There are many uses of the internet that mix multiple functions to great effect. For instance, E-vite, a division of the Interactive Corporation, blends traditional email with a number of other functions. Layered over email in a hypertext form, E-vite provides a 'free' service for people organizing meetings and parties. Identical invitations are sent out to those on the guest list, who are invited to respond not only with whether they are coming but also who might be accompanying them. Added features include the capacity for potential guests and the organizer to view who is coming to the party as it is developing. Also, individual guests can send particular short notes to the organizer that can be collected for the event. E-vite has been successful at becoming part of the organization of the smallest of birthday parties as well as large-scale events. In terms of the internet, it blends: the web with email through its sophisticated hypertext and image-rich original message and links to the specific site for replying to the invitation; email with listservs through its temporary guest list structure; and ultimately online advertising, as each of these paths has the potential to be a site for the placement of advertisements in exchange for its free use. Through electronic organizing, E-vite, which describes itself as the 'world's definitive social planning destination', claims in its 2003 annual report to have hosted via email '2 million events, delivered over 65 million email based invitations' with a monthly average of 5 million users on its website (E-vite, 2004)

Although E-vite has developed a relatively unique service for users of the internet, the activities it facilitates identify the shift in cultural practices into new media cultures. E-vite has infiltrated and integrated a kind of commercial exchange in an arena of activity invested with personal cultural production and at the very heart of communities and groups, and how they maintain their social networks. Birthday parties, one of the most common uses for E-vite, are also the sorts of event that generate a great deal of personal development by individuals and investment by friends. Certainly restaurants and wedding services have developed unique markets through catering for children's birthday parties or the elaborate logistics of some marriage receptions, but it is rare that there has been a coordinating service for organizing the invitation list and the responses for the most everyday and the most intimate of our special occasions.

The internet has profoundly challenged the divides that traditional media have established between production and reception. Our investigation in this chapter is an attempt to unravel the new ways that individuals and groups use the internet. In its many forms, the internet celebrates cultural production. We could call the internet a DIY media form in its invocation to users to fabricate their media practices; but it is important to understand that this development of a DIY media form is not freed from the operations of corporations. The internet has developed into a blended structure in the tradition of E-vite, where personal uses are intertwined with very commercial imperatives. Emerging from this is a new cultural politics that needs to be explored more fully and investigated more intricately. The internet as DIY media form brings to the fore a number of key elements that we will investigate in turn as they manifest themselves on the web. First, as we have emphasized, the internet is focused on production for all its users. Second, the internet presents a new configuration of public and private that is being explored through its variety of communication forms from email and chat to websites and listservs. Third, the internet produces tensions and synergies between capitalism and cultural activity that are complex as they define the new terrain of cultural politics. Each of these elements is heavily intertwined with the others; for the sake of analysis in this chapter, we will explore each of them individually and assess their cultural implications.

Producing the internet's media form: the World Wide Web

Of all the various communication possibilities available via the internet, the development of the World Wide Web was most like a past media form. Even in its less graphically developed stages of the early 1990s, it provided electronic pages of information that could be read. What made it distinctive from other reading material was that the web page contained a means for the user to connect from one site to another web page developed by someone else. Any hyperlink, which traditionally has been designated through underlined text, became the access point to an altogether new website. Thus any particular website was potentially connected to an infinite matrix of other URLs. As a user, this changed the discrete cultural object that was so much part of film production or book publishing into something new that was defined fundamentally by its connection to other locations and sites. Users could begin in one location in their searches and finish somewhere with only the remotest connection to that original starting point.

With these origins of dispersion and interconnection of information and materials, we also have the outline of a different identity of the user involved with the web. The user was unlike an audience member generated by television or film. With the development of the graphic user interface of the web, first with MOSAIC (1993), then Netscape and lastly the prevalence of Microsoft's Internet Explorer, the user became a surfer of graphically rich sites. This graphic internet stage of the web, roughly from late 1993 to 1998, describes a period where the majority of websites were organized around text and image with possibly an animated loop image or gif to add an extra dimension. Thus websites for users resembled glossy magazines in their design and presentation. And they were 'read' with similar levels of surface intensity to their print counterparts. The entire web became an elaborate newspaper of stories and information that the individual pieced together into their own personal selections. To aid in this process of looking for interesting and relevant materials, search engines became the website that many users were drawn to as a first port of call. Lycos and Inktomi, along with a host of other search engines, provided the techniques to connect to related sites in the graphic internet stage of the web (Marshall, 1997). Yahoo! was also highly successful in organizing weblinks via categories of interest. America Online (AOL) constructed an internal network of connection through its keyword search technique, which would only bring up sites that were part of its family of content providers. In all cases, the user was offered an excess of possible sites with almost any search. As opposed to the scarcity model that depended on elaborate systems of gatekeeping of content in traditional media, the web served to break down those barriers in its relatively non-hierarchized representations of websites after any search.

The meaning of this experience for the 'audience' is complex. For one thing, the term audience no longer made sense for most web-related activities. Second, the concept of the user comes closer to the identity that the websurfer inhabits. The former coherence of national broadcasts or even coordinated movie releases as common experiences for the populace was not as possible through the web. Even the postmodern characterization of surface without depth is not an accurate way of describing the web experience; perhaps more than anything else the web allowed for the opposite of surface experience. With its plenitude of information on many subjects, it actually offered greater depth with greater ease of finding that information than ever before.

Developing in the graphic internet stage (1993–98) was a user subjectivity that had some other important attributes (Marshall, 1997). On one level, the user was isolated in his/her experience; after all, no two web-surfing experiences were identical and the use of the personal computer for web browsing helped to ensure the singularity of the activity. On another level, the web experience provided new forms of association that were much more difficult to manifest under old regimes of connection. Websites offered techniques of connection that overcame the problems of distance for the building of associations and communities. Although there have been many debates about the quality of the communities that have emerged from the internet, there is no question that there are new organizations that have 'materialized' from its transnational reach and its capacity to provide infinite content on the most arcane or popular phenomenon. For example, websites as fan sites have proliferated in diversity and sheer numbers from this early era of the web; similarly websites devoted to particular kinds of knowledge, such as medicine, have expanded exponentially over the last decade. Websites dedicated to a particular kind of sport or pastime have become clusters of involvement for those whose own identity is connected to these activities. This sense of the web that is borne from this early excitement about its possibilities could be described as a subjectivity defined by passion. The web provides myriad opportunities for a form of affective investment that has greater significance because the website's existence itself implies that others share the particular passion.

A further attribute of the web user's subjectivity has been fostered by the perceived free quality of the original graphic internet stage. With its origins in universities whose users were given open access and with others connecting to the internet from work or other public places, in the first five years of the web there was a sense that the internet gave entrée to information that was not usually available free of charge. Even though home access was channelled through an internet service provider (ISP) with a monthly fee and/or phone rates, the initial sensation of something for nothing was prevalent throughout web surfing experiences. This sense of something for nothing did not emerge out of a cultural vacuum: a longer history in computer culture has been similarly constructed around a free flow of information. Many variations have emerged from this libertarian sentiment that is wedded to the internet. What has been described as the shareware movement, where developed computer code was openly accessible to others to modify and improve while acknowledging its source through voluntary payments, has been fundamental to many of the software developments and innovations in computer applications (see Europe Shareware, 2004). Open source, which is connected to the non-proprietarial operating system Linux, has represented a perpetual challenge to both Microsoft and Apple's dominance in software development. Organizations such as the Electronic Freedom Foundation, with its original proselytizer John Perry Barlow, represented the political dimension of this general sensibility. Barlow among others argued for the web and the internet to be left alone to develop without government intervention and regulation: with this freedom, the internet and web could develop into a much more ideal community not corrupted by the larger powers and influences (Barlow, 1993; see also Free Software Foundation).

These various strains of understanding the web as free and as a place for the unfettered exchange of information have led to a range of subjectivities that define the web experience. In the least innocuous of these, the user of the web parallels the subjectivity of the library patron. The web acts as a remarkable resource where information can be borrowed and used for personal purposes. With the digitalization of images and text, the difference in that borrowing is that the copy is a perfect replica of the original. What breaks down in the web experience is the origins of material and the authorial control over that material. Nonetheless, the web user as library patron is an idealized conceptualization, however incomplete. Indeed, the diametrically opposed subjectivity of the web user is closer to the pirate, where old regulations of property no longer apply and the web itself is stateless and powerless to prevent what would traditionally have been called theft. The most dramatic and pervasive example of the web user as pirate with all its romanticism intact is with music downloading. Although we will deal with music downloading later in this chapter, it is worth highlighting here how the founder of Napster, Shawn Fanning, represented a modern-day Robin Hood in the collective consciousness. Simultaneously celebrated for the simplicity with which he developed the exchange of music from millions of users (with his image on the cover of *Time* magazine – a tried and true but perhaps tired sign of cultural significance (Greenfeld, 2000)), and painted as a villain by the music corporations. Fanning allowed users to flout and circumvent the cost of corporately produced music CDs.

To put this pirate-like identity back into the wider user subjectivity, it is accurate to say that web use has drawn the user into a new tactical and strategic counter-position to the emerging new economy and its imperatives. In this way, web use and the user is closer to de Certeau's notions of tactical and strategic interventions that sometimes imply a larger political direction, but more often describe that the interests of larger powers and corporations are not necessarily in alignment with the many users (de Certeau, 1984). When one considers that the web is often accessed at work (40 per cent of all use by some estimates (Nielsen Mediametrix, 2004)) for non-work purposes and strategies, it becomes clearer that the web articulates de Certeau's moments of resistance that are pandemic in contemporary culture. Even the prevalence of pornography on the web highlights its use as not necessarily for the informational purposes imagined. This threatening possibility of kinds of knowledge and entertainment not culturally sanctioned has been the motivating force behind both parents' and governments' efforts to regulate the web in some way. The reaction to these efforts at paternalism has been more vociferous, and has concerted efforts to circumvent the controls and programs that contain the use within a country or by a child. Emerging from this wider identity of the pirate is the hacker, an experienced invader and manipulator of computer code who demonstrates their prowess through feats of shutting down powerful corporations. In certain instances, the hacker has a political objective: most viruses and worms are developed to destroy those operating systems supported by Microsoft and one could read their political intention of unseating the monopolistic power of this overarching corporation.

Even this interesting schizophrenic subjectivity of library patron and marauding pirate does not quite encompass the varied structure of identity of the web user. What is missing is that even in the most mundane searches, there is something being produced by the surfer. Axel Bruns has highlighted a second split subjectivity through identifying terms such as 'prosumer' and 'produser' that some researchers have employed to express the new web 'audience' (Bruns, 2002). Part of the web experience is that consumption and reception rival qualities that are closer to production. Though it is a truism that web surfers become readers and viewers that resemble the audiences produced by television and magazines, it is an equal truism that they are drawn to produce their web experiences. This production of the user's entertainment and/or information is a component of the interactive qualities of the web that were developed in chapter two. The web invites us to click on to the next level, the next page, the next link or the next answer. Interactivity in many web structures, then, could be redefined as the interaction between production and consumption. The web user as prosumer leads to all sorts of repercussions, including a reorientation of how information and media companies might use the web for profit. In a sense, the audience has always been an intermediary in what is being produced; now the audience's use is factored in to the actual presentation of the content. Looking at any successful commercial website, one is struck how elaborate its organization of content can be. In other words, even within a particular website there is a plenitude of content and possible different directions to take by the user. Even news has transformed because of the web: there is a greater search quality for information and news by users – what we could identify as informational news (Burnett and Marshall, 2003: 159–70). In other words, they are less dependent on one source and become comfortable in finding information rather than it being provided. The industry in the 1990s began differentiating between media that pushed information at the user as would happen in a television news broadcast and information that was designed to pull the user to move to a new level as it would on a website. Chris Chesher, trying to describe the differences between narrative and CD-ROMs identified the same differentiation: new media invokes you to respond, while older media forms attempt to evoke sentiments (Chesher, 1996). The web has clearly become a technology that invokes us to act and produce our content through our own searches.

In many scenarios, the producer dimension of the user is beyond what we have described as everyday searches. Each day new websites are produced and existing ones are transformed. The top search engines are now indexing over 3 billion web pages. Since the mid-1990s the majority of new websites have been commercial entities; nevertheless, the sheer number of personal websites produced by individuals continues to grow along with the overall size of the web. Although many meanings can be drawn from this explosion of personal websites and some of these will be explored further in the next section, it is evident that the web has catered to a desire in the populace to produce and to make something, and ensure that whatever is produced has the possibility of being seen. The will to produce is certainly not unique to the web. In terms of media forms, the development of the personal camcorder and even super-eight film was designed for home production of video and film. The still camera has had more than a century of use by 'consumers' as they produced images of their families and special occasions. This rich history of production through different media by individuals and not for profit possesses one clear distinction from the production of the website: the web is simultaneously a place for production, distribution and exhibition in a way that no previous media form has ever permitted. The rather severe gatekeeping that worked to determine what and who were permitted to exhibit or broadcast in forms such as film and television was not in operation on the internet and the World Wide Web. It should be made clear that other techniques have been implemented by powerful media and internet corporations to ensure that certain commercial sites attract a greater number of users than a personal website, but it is also important to underline that the potential for attracting audiences by one individual and not a corporation is an ever present sensation and possibility of the web. Some of the most successful internet corporations, such as Yahoo!, began as cataloguing websites designed by two individuals around their personal interests (Burnett and Marshall, 2003, 97).

Much like many other computer-related skills, web authoring has become increasingly more accessible as the software derived from the original codes has developed. Hypertext markup language, or html, is the basic language used to code the script that defines the various features of web pages. Text and images are given html 'tags' or commands that – when the file is loading in a browser such as Netscape or Microsoft Internet Explorer – generate the colours, the design and the graphics that produce the sophisticated look of web pages. It is the high-quality design that has made website production such a compelling medium for so many to develop their individual websites. With relatively little effort, a web page can look as polished as a national glossy magazine. One of the features of learning to make web pages is that any web page that already exists can be copied and used as raw material for the development of a new page: the source code is all in place. This process of appropriation to both learn the html codes and master the new techniques of making websites has been used extensively by individuals. Source code is used and re-used ad infinitum. Moreover, software such as Dreamweaver can further simplify the integration of text, image and moving image into the structure of a site. More difficult coded sources such as Flash and Fireworks, along with Adobe Photoshop, are becoming commonplace on desktop computers for the development of websites. Even those disinclined to develop their skills with new computer software can simply save a word-processing file in html code. The most difficult procedure beyond making the website is developing a competency in uploading and downloading the various connected pages that the individual has constructed. Considering that most free email services provide both techniques and space for posting a website, hosting one is a challenge that is within the grasp of millions of web users. The limitations for the production of websites can be economic. Much like many consumer-developed 'production' activities, from home renovation to home videos, from gardens to art and craft work, the will-to-produce has become the domain of the middle class – though not exclusively by far. Viewed cynically, personal websites represent the most mundane of aspirations to be something more; but understanding the aspirational quality that is part of these productions allows us to understand more accurately how new media forms are permitting an exploration of production through production and how that sentiment is not limited to particular class fractions. The will to produce is a pervasive cultural phenomenon that is elemental to the appeal of new media and the cultures it has spawned.

The transforming public sphere

The idea of the public sphere has been very much wedded to the kinds of media that have been utilized, and the types and locations of discussion that were produced within any culture. Jürgen Habermas, in defining the public sphere, pointed to a particular time – late eighteenth- and early nineteenth-century Europe – where a vibrant public sphere developed which debated the issues of the day (Habermas, 1989). This public sphere was dependent on the publication of tracts, nascent newspapers, and books, as well as a location to read and further the discussion of their value. Coffee houses, reading rooms and cafes in nineteenth-century France to a degree defined Habermas's conceptualization of sites for the development of a public discussion both by providing the location of the reading material and the place where ideas could be explored in conversation. Although Habermas's interpretation of the public sphere has been criticized for representing a much too narrow fragment of the population, particularly with the virtual exclusion of women, an active public sphere has generally been seen as a requisite for the operation of democratic societies. His work went on to describe how the emerging media and its organization in twentieth-century culture served to produce a decline in active public sphere so that key interests could be overlooked and an ideology that only supported capitalism could flourish in this vacuum of energized discussion and eventual political action.

If nothing else, the internet has been heralded as a place for a new transformation of the public sphere. As some writers have pointed out, Habermas's conceptualization of a single public sphere overlooked the idea that multiple and intersecting publics could be operating within a culture and be developing new ideas and new political directions based on their smaller orbit of connection (see Robbins, 1993). Although various writers have argued that television developed all sorts of new political directions from its different constitution and evocation of an audience, the internet in its range of methods of communication has produced many active and invested publics in a much more obvious and politically engaged way.

In 2003, the effect of the internet on contemporary American politics was felt viscerally. Howard Dean, a Democratic Party presidential candidate and former Governor of Vermont developed a campaign that moved him from relative obscurity to national prominence via very pointed use of the internet as a way to connect to his growing body of supporters. His campaign moved beyond contacting potential supporters via email; it attempted to involve his supporters in the building of the meaning of the campaign itself. Supporters were encouraged to be part of discussion groups that were read closely by the campaign manager and Dean himself as they gleaned how the ideas of Dean had stimulated a growing cluster of interest. This interest led to financial support from hundreds of thousands of small donors, a type of financing that raised more than $40 million and well in excess of any other Democratic candidate. His campaign gradually focused on opposition to the 2003 Iraq War, which was particularly valuable in connecting to younger voters who were very comfortable in using the internet as a communication medium that could generate large connections as well as small communities.

Dean's campaign had an official weblog, which provided an insider's view of the campaign as it toured across the country, and it encouraged an elaborate web ring for others to write about their experiences at a more grassroots level in connecting to potential voters. In the lead-up to the American primaries that select the party's candidate, Dean became the front-runner in December 2003 and early January 2004. Part of his success in using the internet led to the involvement of a whole new group of Americans previously excluded from the political process. His method of connecting to his supporters was to empower them as integral to the meaning of the campaign. This sense of empowerment was possible because the means of contact via the internet's various communication modes allowed for people to have a sense of both investment and solidarity in the common cause. The internet provided a classic blending of an almost personal connection between the candidate and the supporter as well as a means to present a public version of the candidate for wider consumption. The website functioned as an entrée into this particular world of Howard Dean and his political directions, and represented the most public version. The weblog with its more 'insider' personal register allowed the supporter the sense of belonging. With the campaign encouraging people to contribute to the 'blog' and to begin their own sites and related blogs devoted to his election an elaborate network of related interest developed. The website entreated people to work towards a number of strategies of inclusion: donations, setting up local groups, and staying in touch with supporters from different states and different interest groups that supported Dean. A group celebrating youth support for Dean, calling itself GenDean and with its own website (www.generationdean.com), claimed 22,479 members and 1333 groups. On the official weblog, hundreds of links provided an elaborate but interconnected web ring of supporters. The site also indicated that 640,000 people were supporters and encouraged everyone to join the '$100 Revolution' where small contributions from a massive number of supporters millions could be generated. Part of the appeal of Dean's internet campaign was its capacity to update daily. Augmented by opening the possibility for personal expression as testimonials generally, the internet campaign blended beautifully the public development of a politician with the more private but publicly expressed testaments by individuals. With supporters writing opinions and perpetually conversing and updating websites there was the genuine sense of producing and making what was an election campaign into a stronger political reality.

Although Dean's campaign for the presidency ultimately faltered as it moved from his dedicated supporters and organizers to the wider Democratic Party constituency and a presentation of himself via television, it was nonetheless, a remarkable organization of political will derived from a clear knowledge of the way that the internet can produce a sense of intimate connection even around the largest of public issues and the presentation of public personalities.

The internet can be seen as part of a larger cultural shift in the delineations and meanings of public and private. Although these shifts in contemporary culture predate the internet, the new media form allowed for a further exploration of the private in a public forum. For instance, webcams became a particularly popular means of expressing sometimes the most private sphere in the most public way. One of the original and most popular webcam sites was JenniCam operated by Jennifer Ringley, started while she was a college student and self-confessed 'computer geek'. Here is how she explained her site in 2003, seven years after its launch:

> The 'JenniCam' is, in essence, a series of cameras located throughout the house I live in with my partner Dex and a small herd of animals. These cameras take images in this house all day long, every day… This site is a look through the virtual windows into my home. I don't act, play for, or really even pay attention to the cameras. I don't put on a show for you. But by the same token, I don't censor the cameras.

> (Discontinued site)

From its launch, JenniCam made Jennifer Ringley a celebrity. Newspapers and magazines ran cover stories and anchored their coverage of the web and the internet with this brazen example of making one's private universe available for public consumption. The site attracted thousands of subscribers and devotees over the years – by her own estimation she was receiving more than a million hits a week. Although she closed down her site in early 2004, its success over the years led many others to imagine that webcams were a means of crossing the virtual proscenium arch: the former audience members could now become stars of their own perpetual series. There are now elaborate webcam rings that present similar profiles of individual's inner sanctums. Subscriptions have developed and many of the webcam rings are now closely linked to pornography. It is true that webcams serve many other purposes – for instance, just marking a particular street corner or beach location to advertise the site as a travel destination. Nonetheless, personal webcams dramatically represent the blending of public display in private locations that embodies the web experience.

The internet has simultaneously heralded a new age of voyeurism, narcissism and exhibitionism, all within its various forms. Surveillance has also exited the world of internet webcams to become the organizing narrative of reality television around the world. This extended world of exposure is partly related to the ubiquitousness of the camera and the capacity to distribute the images presented. It is equally about a changed relationship to media and presentation that proliferates and generates more and more personal websites, webcams and commercial sites that play with the idea of looking in on private worlds. This new voyeurism in its twinned relationship to exhibitionism is fundamentally different than that developed via film and video where the audience members projected their identities on to the larger-than-life screen images. Via the internet, the everydayness of personal and intimate images that are perpetually accessible has transformed the cultural discourse of what is public and what is private, who is the performer and who is the audience.

Within this mix of public and private that the web has produced, the internet has led to a variety of communication forms that have drawn massive participation. Chatrooms, which are dependent on the relatively simple technology of internet relay chat (IRC), allow participants to engage in text-based real-time conversations. What has made this form another challenge to our divides between public and private space is the ease with which one can join chatrooms and communicate about some of the most intimate details of one's life. The transcendence of reserve is partly permissible because of the anonymity of any sender in the chat, and writers such as Turkle (1995) and Markham (1998) among many others have written about how anonymity permits a floating identity in cyberspace. Indeed, notorious stories of false identities populate the first ten years of widespread internet use. Moral panics around children being drawn to meet fellow chatroom participants (adults posing as children) has surfaced as a regular story in television crime drama as much as newspaper articles.

In a more general sense, the internet has provided the means to engage in forms of interpersonal communication that permit time and space manipulation of the interaction. Traditionally, interpersonal communication is thought of as face to face in format and can be structured around dialogues and multilogues or conversations. Email, which can be used almost for broadcasting a particular message through sending that message to millions, is generally a technique of dialogue (one to one). It is, however, 'asynchronous' – that is, the responses are not at the same time and thus the form of interpersonal communication is mediated by a time difference in response. Internet relay chat, in contrast, tries to replicate the synchronous quality of communication. In order to speed up that connection, responses are often very short and filled with emoticons and acronyms of frequently used expressions (a technique that has been further refined in mobile phone text messaging). Because of this time compression, chats emulate the interpersonal nature of phone conversations and face-to-face communication. Many researchers have been drawn to the effects of this new variation on interpersonal communication. For some of the subjects in Annette Markham's research, the lack of face-to-face interaction was liberating: one is no longer judged by appearances (Markham, 1998: 172–5). Identities become connected to how well you express your sentiments and argue your points and friendships, and liaisons build from that basis. Other researchers have worked to determine whether internet chat makes the least sociable dependent on its apparently isolating experience for their interactions. Findings have generally indicated that chat and other internet communication forms are just as likely to reinforce friendships developed externally as they are to build new virtual friendships. The internet reinforces the strong interpersonal bonds among family members and existing social ties, particularly those separated by distances (Pew Project, 2000). As developed in chapter three, the intertwining nature of public and private networks that define the internet is permitting the development of new cultural groups and attachments. Hundreds of thousands of chatgroups work to exclude new members as much as they endeavour to reinforce a sense of belonging to those that already participate. Fan networks have been strengthened by the combination of websites and usegroups attached to very specific and niche interests. Politically inspired movements are possible with the internet in defying the problems of distance between their active members. The recent phenomenon of flash mobs or gatherings, where a group of people connected via that internet suddenly appear at a particular location in a given city, emphasizes the power of the internet to form connected and highly invested interest communities that can move seamlessly from the virtual to the real world (Kahney, 2003).

The weblog articulates this different composition of the various new media cultures that are emerging. At first glance, the weblog is simply a form of narcissism: but more accurately, it is another way an individual produces their identity. Much like how a front garden can be an expression of the occupants of a house, or how a mantelpiece or bookshelf is designed to reveal the identity of its owner, the weblog is an elaborate presentation of the self. The technology that is part of new media cultures, however, celebrates that production of the self in forms that were once the preserve of the media industry. With the weblog, the personal website with all its meanderings becomes a public testament, a proclamation of significance and an expression of individuality. At the same time, many weblogs are interconnected into rings where interests intersect and overlap and the individual quality of the weblog belongs much more to a linked social fabric. The personal weblog is a cultural feature of the landscapes of new media that expresses the desire to produce and the utilization of the most ready material for that production. Weblogs rely on the everyday experiences of their writers and their will to 'narrativize' those experiences. Along with personal websites and webcam sites, weblogs represent the desire and the outcome of the production ethos that prevails in new media cultures. As in Stuart Allan and Barbie Zelizer's investigations of immediate post-11 September New York, these apparent personal accounts became the raw material for the expression of the news event as the personal production became the source for countless journalistic stories (Allan and Zelizer, 2002). That particular moment led to the emergence of the public weblog produced by columnists for major media outlets: the blog as a form of expression moved from new media diary to public forum that was part of older media forms.

The complex role of capital

Despite the internet's pedigree as a technology developed by government, the role of commerce has been part of the emerging cultures that have developed through the internet's various forms of communication. Indeed, government's involvement in the 1990s in many countries was motivated by a desire to develop the commercial quality of the internet. For instance, for its first 10 years electronic commerce via the internet was exempt from American taxation. In the United States, Al Gore's National Information Infrastructure (NII) was as much about a programme to ensure access to the populace as it was to build the necessary networks to facilitate an information economy boom.

As we have described above, two of the key identity tropes for the internet were as library patron and pirate. Both of these identities present a challenge to any commercial imperative for the internet. After all, neither of these identities can be thought of as an ideal consumer identity. In fact, one of the key challenges of the internet is that production is so dispersed among the millions of users that it is difficult to construct the value of particular information. As a result, the economy of the internet has taken many detours in producing profits. Countless internet businesses have failed because people have come to expect a free quality to internet service and open-ended possibilities for personal productions in one shape or another.

Estimating the size of the internet economy was part of its development in the 1990s as investors and analysts tried to work out the worth of companies that were trading in the virtual world. Giant e-retailer Amazon only generated its first profits five years after its initial appearance on the stock exchange, which underlines the phantom and future nature of much of the internet's 1990s economic value. In April 2000, there was a severe adjustment in the stock values of many internet companies and technology-related stocks where prices tumbled and thousands of start-up internet businesses disappeared within months or even days. This collapse was generally labelled the bursting of the dotcom economic bubble.

Since that collapse, the internet economy has become less separated from other aspects of industry and normalized as another component. When separating electronic commerce, estimates still put the international economy in excess of $300 billion in revenues and activity. The travel industry has been transformed dramatically by people buying their airline tickets online and is exemplary of this normalization of internet use for certain types of business. Similarly, book retailing was overwhelmed by the eventual success of Amazon. Progressively, other existing businesses have developed an online presence to challenge the emergence of online-only companies. According to Forrester Research, in excess of 10 per cent of company websites are fully interactive for sales and not just promoting or advertising their products and services (Forrester, 2004). Increasingly people are comfortable buying online because of its simplicity and convenience. Advertising in various forms is another immensely profitable element of the internet. Roughly 3 per cent of advertising revenues worldwide are now generated via the internet, giving rise to revenues of $7.2 billion in 2003 according to its own industry board (Interactive Advertising Bureau, 2004).

What has been significant in the development of the internet is this new ground of contestation and cultural struggle between what defines a commodity and therefore becomes part of the domain of the internet economy and what evades that definition of value. With the massive production of websites by individuals and the equally massive production of information on these websites, the commercial dimension has been elusive for companies. It is important to understand this contestation from several key vantage points.

First of all, the economy of the internet cannot be separated from the tools that have allowed users access. With the development of the personal computer, relevant applications became the driving force for individuals and families to buy computers for their homes. One rationale for the purchase of a computer was to facilitate learning by school-age children. Thus software, usually in the form of CD-ROMs, expanded the value of the machine beyond a sophisticated typewriter. Dictionaries, encyclopedias, and drawing and document design software all became part of the meaning of the home computer in the early 1990s. Coupled to this development was the desire to make the home computer an entertainment source to expand its utility. Computer games further expanded the value of the home computer and led many upper-middle-class families to purchase individual computers for each of their children. Alongside the software expansion of the value of the computer was the emergence of the internet. Many ISPs initially offered access to the internet through modem – telephone connection to their bank of servers directly connected to the internet itself. Particularly successful providers such as AOL were able to construct a graphic overlay and an intranet of services and information that kept the user within their network. AOL's success was in its ability to translate the internet and its capacity into a ready-to-use and controlled environment. Each of these kinds of software and graphic interface overlays were designed to increase the accessibility of both the computer and the internet. Their commercial imperative as ISPs was driven by the need to expand their subscriber base; money was not made from the content of the internet, but rather by the numbers of people who were willing to pay a monthly fee for access.

Second, because the internet emerged from government developments (even though its expansion was initially dependent on telephone lines and eventually cables into homes) and was originally used extensively at universities, it maintained a quasi-public service dimension. After all, most countries ensured that their public libraries were connected to the internet so that the widest range of people could participate in the new information-driven culture. The internet resembled a public utility service, which in many countries had traditionally been directly run under a government-controlled agency or was highly regulated by government policy. In either case, even as the internet moved to a much more commercial model by the mid-1990s, this vestigial structure and vision of the internet persisted. As detailed earlier in this chapter, part of the emergence of personal computer culture and its intersection with the internet was a very libertarian notion of its status: the Electronic Freedom Foundation and John Perry Barlow have consistently articulated that the internet has to be an open and free space for activities.

Third, as a way to maintain the free quality of the emerging internet, the web and other services have become inundated with advertisements. The objective of any internet-driven business now resembles any television or radio network: evidence of as many people as possible viewing the website so that their viewing can be sold on to advertisers. On television, the enticing and apparent 'free lunch' for watching all of the commercials is the actual programme. On the Internet, the equivalent 'free lunch' provided to users are services such as email. For example, Hotmail expanded rapidly to over 100 million users by 2001 as word spread virally about its ease of use and its capacity to connect to other users. Surrounding any Hotmail email are advertisements that are tagged to the correspondence. Similar structures surround Yahoo! accounts or Google searches. In some cases, search results reflect the desires of particular advertisers, where companies pay to be located in the top ten for particular search words. The internet has become a much more mature media form and generally has acquiesced to the presence of advertisements to keep the information ostensibly 'free'. What this has done is clog the arteries of the internet with extraneous information and make it much more like the space in a shopping mall. Nielsen supports this transformation of the internet by aggregating internet use from its surveys. Like television ratings, websites are bestowed value by the number of 'hits' they receive. These hits translate into advertising rates per thousand hits.

Paying for information without advertising has been decidedly less successful on the internet as advertising has become pervasive in all its transparent and timed pop-up windows. There are exceptions to this pattern of the internet. Pornography has had enormous success at getting users to pay. With elaborate 'free' previews, pornography sites are also quick to sell their 'viewers' to other pornography sites in a perpetual game of pop-up windows. Likewise, business information about companies and about trends in particular industries has had reasonable success at getting patrons to pay for information. These remain exceptions to the general rule of the 'freeness' of the internet – if we overlook the large sums collected through connection fees by the ISPs.

Finally, as much as the internet has become commercialized and has succumbed to the patterns of revenue and profit generation that are endemic to our contemporary media, it has also permitted new forms of contestation that have become foundational to understanding new media cultures. One of the features of digitalized products is that they have become much easier to copy. Moreover, the copy is a replica of the original with no real loss in quality. As described above, one of the key identities of the internet user is that of the pirate. This identity has emerged most strongly in music file sharing. Napster, the internet site developed by Shawn Fanning, was one of the first programs to facilitate copying music files from any computer connected to the site. Napster provided an elaborate directory of music available to be copied by the individual user. Some 30 million users of Napster made it the largest loose community of file sharing that one could imagine, all with an interest in getting music files to load on to their computers and into their MP3 players. The movement of music was extraordinary and other sites, such as Kazaa and Morpheus, continued the music file swapping after Napster had been legally closed down and resurfaced as a subsidiary of BMG Music.

This elaborate exchange of music was a challenge to the conventions of ownership and intellectual property. In the past, music sharing and copying was tolerated when it was done between friends. The internet allowed the category of 'between friends' to expand exponentially into millions. And what once appeared harmless – the individual who allows his music to be copied by someone else is not profiting from the transaction – suddenly begins to challenge one of the foundations of the media industry and capitalism more generally: intellectual property rights. Similar exchanges have occurred with films and television programmes; however, the download time without broadband connection made the exchange much more time-consuming and difficult to become more widely utilized. Nonetheless, fileswapping is an outcome of the digitalization of entertainment forms and the expansion of the technology of the internet to connect individuals into elaborate interest communities that are not attached to the exigencies of any element of the entertainment industry. The cultures of new media have made intellectual property one of the terrains of contestation in contemporary culture.

Conclusion

This chapter has surveyed the most converged of media and how it has reshaped the audience into new categories of identity and media use. The internet has highlighted the will-to-produce and the idiosyncratic and sometimes intimate productions that have emerged from its multifaceted communication forms through its millions of users. The reverberations of this dramatic shift in control of the representation of culture and cultural activity are still resonating as much as forming elements of new media cultures. Loose communities have developed that, in some cases such as music file swapping, have challenged the organization of consumer capitalism. Other internet communities have defined themselves as political entities and forces that are leading to change in our polities. Large media corporations have worked to assert their dominance in this new field of activity, partly through their sheer size and partly through their capacity to add technological features that cannot be matched by the everyday productions that occur on the internet. The internet has engulfed a great number of activities and forms within its various structures of distribution and presentation; but what may be more significant is an even closer study of the moments of instability in cultural power that the internet brought to the fore over the past decade. Cultural access and cultural exclusion continue to operate as a dialectical struggle that has been thrown into sharp relief by the uses made of the internet.

chapter five

Playing game cultures: electronic games

Play, an essential component of human experience, has been under-studied. Although there have been some classic works on play, including Huizinga (1955) and Callois (1979), and there have been many studies of play by researchers in psychology trying to discern its meanings for children, it has not been a major object of investigation in media and cultural studies. With the emergence of electronic games, the idea of play and an analysis of its complicated relationship to everyday life has catapulted it centre stage. This chapter aims to explore how electronic games in all their various incarnations are presenting play as a central component of contemporary experience that may parallel other forms of entertainment but has significant qualitative differences. The interactive architecture of electronic games, which changes dramatically the cultural experience of games and play, is also investigated. Games present a particularly powerful example of the distinctive kinds of investment and engagement that are part of new media cultures. In their own way, gameplayers enact a form of cultural production in their remaking of the game through play. The chapter works through a reading of gameplay from the perspective of cultural production and finally an interpretation of the kinds of communities that have developed through online gaming.

The term I will use to encompass the various new media games is **electronic games**. What is interesting about electronic games is that they are a form that has spanned and helped converge the technologies of television and the computer as well as challenge their default functions. Thus we think of videogames as console games plugged through cables and played on the television screen. We think of computer games as CD-ROMs that we place and store on personal computers or perhaps that we download from an internet site. Two other forms of electronic games are also part of a history of the converging technologies of television and the computer: the arcade game, with its larger-than-life quality, played in designated entertainment centres and the handheld game with its many incarnations over the last 30 years. Electronic games, in their four major formats, when contrasted with television, represent a major change in the organization of entertainment in our culture. In economic terms alone, the electronic game industry easily surpasses, in revenues and profits, film industry. Worldwide sales in 'entertainment' software according to the British Department of Trade and Industry had already reached $21 billion by 2001 (Erard, 2004: E6). One survey indicated that 50 per cent of Americans six years and older had played some electronic game in the past year (ESA, 2003). That number of players is said to be higher in countries such as Korea and Japan. Its impact transforms our use of time for leisure pursuits. Electronic games, once thought to be the province of children are now, as J.C. Herz has aptly pointed out, a normal and everyday experience for the more than two generations or 50 million Americans that are now in adulthood, 'whose memory and imagination have been colored by Atari, Nintendo and Sega, the same way that the memory and imagination of previous generations were tinted by television, cinema and vinyl records' (Herz, 1997: 1).

Work and play: a cultural history of computer and videogames

One of the tropes of new media cultures is that there has been a change in the division between work and non-work. As detailed in chapter three, in order to encourage new information workers to work long hours, workspaces have transformed into play spaces. The American university dormitory or residence life has become a model for the organization of work. Similarly for the information classes home spaces have become workspaces as greater parts of homes are now dedicated to computer/internet workstations.

The current incarnation of the home computer, then, embodies this ambivalence and duality around work and play. Contained on the hard drives are the spreadsheets and word-processed files of work along with computer games such as *FIFA World Cup*.

The connection between work and play in new media has a long history that is intimately part of the development of electronic games. The origins of games more generally have an even longer lineage in human history. Games operate in a transitional space. They are outside of regular activities, yet often they stand in for or reconstruct potential experiences. This transitional quality of games is the reason why they are seen as so central to child development. Games structure play into rule-based order that becomes some variation of social structures. Sport with all its patterning in terms of teams and rules is emblematic of war and territoriality. Think of the way that American football or rugby operate as games that ritualistically gain and lose territory. The ultimate war game is chess in its elaborate designation of positions and roles within an epic battle of capturing the opposing side's king. Games also translate the stakes into something more everyday and less threatening. In this way games such as Monopoly serve particular socialization functions in dealing with others as much as understanding the power of money in society. Games' ubiquity in all cultures indicate that their role is beyond that of child development and they serve as something much more substantial than mere pastimes, diversions or leisure pursuits.

The earliest electronic games were very much part of the development of computer technology. Part of the history of the mainframe computer that emerged post-Second World War was testing their computational abilities through solving chess problems. Chess programs developed quickly and competitions between chess players and computers emerged by the 1970s. However it was not until 1997 that a chess program could beat a grand master in a series of matches. Because of this focus on chess, electronic chess games were one of the earliest standalone computer games. Chess served as a way to exit the algorithms and matrices of computer programs and languages, and apply them to simple and straightforward mathematical possibilities. Playing the game via the computer was actually very useful for developing computer language and computer coding in their efforts to reach a form of artificial intelligence.

Official histories of the development of electronic games vary somewhat; but what is clear in their emergence is that the programmers were originally involved in working through other problems. For many of these computer-related problems, games were an indirect way to solve the problem of the lack of display of computer activities. The cathode ray tube terminal that we now associate with computers was not part of its origins. Instead punch cards and elaborate printed computations were the only visual evidence of computer work. In 1958 William Higinbotham, while trying to come up with an exhibition for the Brookhaven National Laboratory, developed the first primitive game that allowed people to manipulate with a knob and button a blip on a radar screen vaguely like a game of tennis (Poole, 2000: 29). His intentions were to make his machines come alive for the public and the game was a popular exhibit over the next two years before it was dismantled (Herman, 1997). Parallel developments occurred at MIT in 1962. Steve Russell in the Engineering Department of MIT worked with the new PDP-1 computer, which included switches and a cathode ray tube for display. He was intrigued by the possibilities of expanding the utility of the display screen beyond inputting data. And, in that sense of play, he developed a game called *Spacewar*. Through using keyboard functions and laying a background of night-sky starry, duelling rockets attempted to shoot each other and avoid the deadly gravitational pull of the sun (Poole, 2000: 30–1; Herz, 1997: 5–8, still available at http://lcs.www.media.mit .edu/groupd/el/projects/spacewar/).

Neither of these early prototypes was made into commercial properties. *Spacewar* was left to be copied and circulated to virtually every major research institution nationally and internationally. It became a pastime of computer programmers and engineers, who often fiddled with its basic structure in an attempt to improve the game. Other computer games developed in similar fashion. *Lunar Lander* became popular with students, computer programmers and researchers in the 1970s: players would attempt to land the lunar module on the moon through carefully manipulating the key strokes that governed the speed of descent, the reverse thrusters and the tilt of the craft. Like its predecessor, *Lunar Lander* helped programmers fill the hours of work with some hours of play. The repercussions of games like *Spacewar* and *Lunar Lander* are neatly summarized by Steve Russell:

> I think the thing I take the most pride in about Spacewar is that it got so many people hooked on computer programming. It caught a lot of eyes and got a lot of interesting people asking, 'How do you do that?'
>
> (Herz, 1997: 8)

The intersection between programmers and games continued in all sorts of different directions. As ARPAnet – precursor to the internet – developed, programs and games were freely distributed among researchers. Fan-like interest in science-fiction novels, films and television programmes was exchanged as often as scientific research in the 1970s and 1980s. Into that mix were added attempts by scientific researchers to develop games that played on these science and fantasy interests. Early versions of text-based games with complicated instructions included *Hammurabi*, *Advent* and *Hunt the Wumpus*. These served as versions of the complicated role-playing games such as *Dungeon and Dragons* that were facilitated by internet connections to become multi-user domains (MUDs) by the 1980s (Herz, 1997: 9–11).

The commercialization of electronic games: home, arcade and amusement park

With the origins of electronic games firmly ensconced in the small research culture of universities where aspiring graduate students played while they developed programming skills, it became difficult to imagine how these games could move beyond a few thousand players into a commercially viable industry. These early games were dependent on gargantuan mainframe computers to operate. However, by 1970, the microchip and microprocessor with their capacity to be programmed in any way, much like a computer, and their ability to store data in a much smaller unit led to some new possibilities in developing electronic games and other commercial applications such as the personal calculator (Gere, 2002: 116).

Certain entrepreneurs worked on bringing that technology out of the research institute and into the home. Because electronic games predated the home computer by well over a decade, the first commercial generation of electronic games was designed to attach to television sets. Nolan Bushnell founded the game company Atari and though his first venture, an arcade game called *Computer Space*, failed, his second game with all the simplicity of the original oscilloscape computer game, entitled *Pong*, was massively popular after its commercial release in 1972 (Poole, 2000: 33–4). As early as 1966, Sega, a Japanese company (whose name stood for SErvice and GAmes) was also developing simple game structures (Gere, 2002: 177). By the mid-1970s, *Pong* was not only in every sports club, bar, lounge and pub in North America and Europe, it was also part of the generation of home television games that ran on cassette consoles and add-on screens. With little variation, *Pong* could transform from a tennis-like game to a soccer or hockey game via a different program. The first game console (1975) was made by Magnavox; it was called Odyssey and distributed widely by the giant retailer Sears Roebuck (Gere, 2002: 178).

Because the first generation of electronic games was composed of such simple codes, clones quickly appeared across the industry and led to the flooding of the market. Microchip technology also allowed for the miniaturization of games, and the handheld game market grew from the mid- to late 1970s. As Gere explains, the videogames began to represent the possibilities of digital culture: 'In the 70s, for want of anything better, the image of the video game acted as a metonym for the burgeoning computerization of society and started to appear in mainstream media as such' (2002: 178). Their ubiquity predated the personal computer as emblems of a transforming culture. Emerging in the late 1970s was the arcade hit *Space Invaders*, which eventually led to the *New England Medical Journal* reporting a new condition entitled '*Space Invaders* wrist' (Herz, 1997: 15).

Rapidly changing markets, the frequent development of clones, and the burnout effect of games themselves on users led to an industry that went through a number of booms and busts. By 1983, the industry was worth over $3 billion. By 1985, it had contracted dramatically to be valued at $100 million (Herz, 1997: 39). With each successive hardware transformation, past games become valueless as players bought the new console and sought new compatible games. Thus Atari floundered when Nintendo's console became dominant; likewise Sega struggled for market share with the emergence of Sony PlayStation in 1995 and Microsoft's X-Box in 2001. In the early era of electronic games, the industry was very much attached to the toy industry's cycles as different fads enveloped the form and died away matching that particular generation of players' exit from adolescence. The new economy of electronic games is vastly different and differentiated.

In terms of platforms, the computer game market has the most adult demographic. The average age of the computer game purchaser and player is 29 in the United States, the largest market (ESA, 2003). The game-console player, with its attendant technology attached to televisions is generally younger and hovers around the pre-teen to teenage age group. The youngest of players is now the handheld market. In the last decade, handheld games have included *Pokémon* from Nintendo and other games with Game Boy (GameCube was its console mate) maintaining a steady flow of new users, and new and updated games. Arcade games have the most complicated demographic. Because of the successive generations of players, the arcade is often a mixed location with older players and teenagers. Older players use the arcade as a break from work at lunch or after hours. Teenagers use the arcade as much as a social setting as a place for games. This dual market has also shifted in some cities: progressively there is a cross-integration of games with entertainment centres where pinball and video arcade games are in close proximity to paintball game locations and laser tag venues.

The breadth of electronic games is difficult to limit to these four platforms. For most of the 1980s and 1990s, arcades were generally the venue for platform experimentation in the development and selling of elaborate new games where concerted attempts were made to add to the sensorial impact of games. For instance, Sega developed several locations including Tokyo, London and Sydney for Segaworld, a theme park with many interactive games and simulated rides. Because of financial hardships partly engendered by the failure of its Dreamcast console, Sega no longer operates the overseas amusement parks; it does, however, continue to have a thriving chain of entertainment centres in Japan. Theme parks, from Disney World to the Australian MovieWorld are arcades writ large. Their ultimate rides over the last decade have tried to simulate movie scenes within rooms that add motion to overwhelming moving images and 360-degree sound. On smaller scales, large-scale simulated race car games have developed: individuals in full-size vehicles compete with others; giant video screens position the location of the driver on the track and ultimately a winner is declared who reaches the virtual finish line represented by its screen image. Over the last decade, the arcade and amusement centre have been the sites for new versions of virtual-reality games. Simulated skiing or snowboarding are some of the most common versions of these games: players are invited to mount a moveable 'board' as they navigate their way down a hill by leaning and balancing on the board. Full virtual-reality games were in vogue in the late 1990s and demanded competing players to don a headset and gun to compete in the virtual space of the game.

The economic impact of electronic games has also meant that the entertainment industry more widely is affected by trends emerging in gaming. Since the 1980s, Hollywood has mined games as a source for its own new narratives. Some such as *Tron* (1982) are extensions of the gaming experience. Other such as *Lawnmower Man* (1992) are extensions of the interactive and immersive sensation of games taken to the level of horror. A vast majority are simply based on electronic games and try to work the brand visibility into yet another product. *Super Mario Bros* (1993) and *Street Fighter* (1994) represent some of the earlier efforts to cross-promote a film out of its status as an electronic game. The most successful cross-over hit in film is *Lara Croft: Tomb Raider* (2001), which built from the game's enormous popularity over several versions. One of the least successful films was also the most audacious: *Final Fantasy* (2001) transformed the game into the first complete digitally animated feature film. The technical achievement with its uncanny construction of human figures created temporary moments of thinking the animation was real; however the film failed because of its lumbering story line that translated into stolid if beautiful images.

What is emerging from this synergy with Hollywood film and the strength of the game industry to influence the film industry, is that certain characters that were established in games are developing allegiances with their audience/players in a way that was once the preserve of television and film. *Mario*, for instance, defines Nintendo games as a brand as much as Mickey Mouse is emblematic of Disney. Likewise, Sega's *Sonic the Hedgehog* has a value as a convertible piece of intellectual property in the same way as Warner Brothers' Bugs Bunny. Game manufacturers, as Jonathan Dee recounts, are beginning to exercise their clout across the entertainment industry (Dee, 2003). Popular music is now placed in games – especially those games that are connected to a musical subcultural style. Product placement, a now routine form of promotion through film and television, is currently a successfully sought-after revenue line for electronic games.

Finally, one of the major differences between electronic game production 20 years ago and today is the actual cost of production per individual game. No longer is it acceptable to produce a game without three-dimensional rendering of the images. Thus the tasks of coding the range of possibilities of games, but also the various artists – from those who work on two dimensions (texture artists) to three dimensions (modellers) – make game production expensive just in terms of sheer workforce and time. Some games are also accompanied with extensive animation sequences and acting talent for these movie trailer-like productions. Further voice-over talent is used throughout the repetitive elements of gameplay. Production of games can take up to a year and have crews that resemble a motion picture credit list. Their costs now exceed $1.5 million (US) for a major game. In addition, game companies are likely to buy the rights to particular films and other forms of popular culture to turn into games. Just as film has drawn on games for its sources, game companies have matched their releases with the marketing push of a major motion picture. For instance, the resurrected Atari Corporation bought the rights to the *Matrix* and even employed the film directors –

Larry and Andy Wachowski – and the acting talent to add new live action sequences to the game (Dee, 2003). The final production costs for the *Into the Matrix* game were $20 million (Herold, 2003).

Gameplay: genres

As the electronic game industry has matured, certain genres have developed. Genres connect expectations by the player with those of the producers, and help organize the markets and the pleasures derived from games. Briefly, here are the principal genres of electronic games.

Simulation: As the name implies, these games try to simulate something for virtual play. They emerged from flight simulators and range from incredibly accurate tank and aircraft control simulation to car, boat, snowboard and ski racing.

Role playing: Unlike simulation games, role playing has emerged from board games and the original *Dungeons and Dragons*. Although they are not all inspired by something gothic or medieval, they have emerged as the older version of networked computer games in multi-user domains (MUDs) and have been studied extensively in terms of their construction of particular internet communities (Turkle, 1995; Markham, 1998; Pargman, 2000).

Strategy: Like role-playing games, strategy games owe their lineage to board games and pit the player against the computer, other players or the limits of the game itself. Often these games are called god-games because the player could control millions of 'virtual' lives in their negotiation and play with building their world, their civilization, their city or suburb. Because of the complexity and the need to play these games over a number of hours, they have tended to be more computer-based games.

Adventure: Games that set up a mission or a quest are often called adventure games. These range from children's games to the bestselling CD-ROM *Myst*, which was designed for all ages. Hybrid versions of these games have developed, such as the *Tomb Raider* series, which incorporates action with the quest. Like strategy games, these games have sold better but not exclusively as computer games.

Fighting/action games: The greatest controversies around games have emerged from these so-called shoot-em-up games. The player is often portrayed in the 'first person' where only their arm and guns are visible as they move through the particular space killing enemies. In fighting games, there is a martial arts flavour to the type of fights although this is massively embellished with new moves and forms of knocking out or killing your opponent. Action games are closely linked to science fiction but not exclusively. Fighting/action games suit both the console and computer platform for playing and have been very successfully adapted to multiplayer online gaming.

Sports: Sports games are really a subgenre of simulation games. As a player you can represent a team or an individual depending on the type of sport and at this stage most major sports have an electronic version. Even country-specific games such as Australian rules football can be played virtually. The key value of any of these games is realism and the opportunity for the gameplayer to simulate being part of major professional sports and teams; in some ways it is a simulation of televised versions of sport in terms of camera angles, commentators and the general look of these games.

Platform: Many of the original videogames from the 1970s and 1980s were games where the player controlled a character that moved horizontally across the screen and, after conquering and overcoming certain obstacles and enemies, would achieve a new level of play or new platform. *Super Mario, Donkey Kong, Sonic the Hedgehog* and *Crash Bandicoot* have all emerged from the two-dimensional horizontal game structure of platform games to their current three-dimensional structure. Platform games are generally designed as family entertainment. Because these games are connected to children, the key characters have been developed outwards into animated television series and (in the case of *Pokémon*) movies and thus are used to brand companies such as Nintendo and Sega in a manner similar to the way Mickey Mouse is used to represent Disney.

Puzzle games: The most weakly commercialized genre of electronic games is commonly known as the puzzle game. The most famous puzzle game is *Tetris* where the player has to continually fit awkward-shaped blocks on top of each other to fill up a shaft. Most of these games have become those that are bundled into computers when purchased or have long been associated with shareware and are therefore virtually free. Puzzle games, however, do sometimes become part of adventure games in order to intensify the mystery and challenge of finding places and things. Over their history, puzzle games have also been well adapted into handheld games and are now regular components of, or downloadable onto, mobile phones.

Traditional games: An often overlooked category of electronic games are those that have been converted into electronic form from board games. Thus you can find versions of Monopoly and chess in electronic form along with backgammon and chequers. Because computer screens are usually organized for one user, these games have had limited success as standalone properties. Once they became staples of online sites connected to large institutional sites such as Yahoo!, they developed massive numbers of loyal users that have become dedicated to their games. Generally these games are two-player games and online variations of board games such as *Literati* (which is a transformed word game in the Scrabble tradition) now have enormous followings internationally. Players are ranked in games such as *Literati* and chess; online tournaments are regular special features; and chat among players is standard.

'Edutainment' games: Because using computers is seen as a necessary skill for young people, games have been developed that blend education use with game strategies. Maths and language 'quest' games are common in the genre, where learning is attached to discovering letters, numbers or word sequences – depending on the skill and age level of the game's design (Herz, 1997; Marshall, 2001).

Gameplay: interaction, cybernetics and cultural production

In all these genres of electronic games, there is a level of interactivity that separates games from other forms of entertainment culture. For the child who owns a *Neopet*, an electronic toy that demands to be fed and taken care of or it will 'run away', there are relentless demands of pet maintenance to attend to that come from the game itself. For other games, the player may be pitted against the machine or against another player or possibly against a host of players. In these various scenarios, which occur primarily in first-person shooter, role-playing and simulation games, the range of interactions moves from the structure of the machine to human-to-human interaction that is mediated by the game. Interactivity becomes increasingly complex as the human-to-human interaction becomes a central feature of the pleasure of the game itself. Interactivity in these games becomes a kind of cultural production albeit contained within the framework of the game's rules.

Lev Manovich rightly underlines that the game's interactivity is highly structured by the game's programmer and the player is not creating freely but within this limited world (Manovich, 2001). This critique presents games as ultimate cybernetic systems: rules cannot be broken, and the goals and objectives of the game can rarely, if ever, be challenged or changed within a game. Thus if the objective of *Wolfenstein* or *Doom* is to kill the enemy, there is no opportunity to change its rules to build in clever diplomatic negotiations to avoid bloodshed. For gameplayers working within a given genre who accept the game's and genre's rules, this challenge would be absurd partly because it destroys the pleasure of the game itself. Nonetheless, the cybernetic critique of games is powerful, particularly when it is taken as leading to the potentially limited worldview that may be proffered via games for players.

The cybernetic critique of electronic games takes on greater credibility when the military's profound and lengthy interest in both the development of games and the utilization of games for training soldiers is factored into our consideration. Flight simulators, long a training tool for pilots, were an invention of both gaming and the military, and developed with electronic display from the 1960s onwards. By 1978, flight simulators had become a standard computer game which has gained in sophistication over the last quarter-century and integrated into the construction of many war-related electronic games. Games have been used in military training to improve reflexes and to accustomize the soldier with the electronic displays of targets and objectives. Most recently, the US Army, through a military academy, developed a very sophisticated multi-level training game entitled *America's Army*. Players move from Fort Benning and basic training to eventually assessing their abilities for Special Forces at Fort Bragg, another training base. Certainly the game glorifies the military and is being used as a sophisticated marketing tool to connect to the core recruiting market in the United States who regularly play electronic games. Indeed, because of a convergence of display technologies from electronic games to the means of controlling military machines from anti-aircraft guns to the operation and firing of tanks, elements of war itself in its hyperreal and mythological conception of precision resembles – deceptively and falsely – electronic games.

The cybernetic quality of games has served as a source of critique for the most violent games. Gruesome real-life shootings in the United States with the 1999 Columbine High School massacre and in Germany with the Urfurt massacre in 2003 by 19-year-old Robert Steinhauser have been linked to the perpetrators' overuse of violent videogames. *Doom* became the *bête noire* because it was seen as the Columbine shooters' favourite game. Critics of violent electronic games indicate that the routine killing in games leads to a general desensitization towards the actions of violence and a specific effect on those that already have a predisposition to violence. This critique is not new and is not unique to electronic games. It has been used for decades against violence on television and violence on cinema screens; however with electronic games the research has a different angle that has allowed for the debate to intensify. In contrast to television, games demand a more intense experience by the gameplayer and repetition of violent action to advance in the game. As a result, the effect of the violence on-screen is greater than in the passive structures of television watching (Anderson and Dill, 2000). Debates about violence in electronic games have mainly circulated around protecting children because games are seen as products in a regulatory sense primarily aimed at youth (even though most games are now bought by people over the age of 18) and it is a truism in the industry that violence levels become a kind of selling feature. To counter this development the games industry has attempted to self-regulate through providing warnings and buying guidelines for games. Despite these efforts, the debate about whether screened violence is compartmentalized by players and viewers remains an endless and seemingly irresolvable issue.

Although the objectives of games may be simple (for example, the common 'kill or be killed' in first-person shooter games) and structured by game designers, there is no question that games are compelling for players. The sensation that games are controlling players is an extension of the cybernetic critique of games: a popular reading of games is to call them addictive. Players are drawn into a pleasure of repetition in the long struggle to master the game. Game manufacturers have constructed levels to differentiate and provide gradations of skill for game players to gauge their progress. Parents battle this play compulsion where they feel they must limit the time that children spend playing games. As Grodal relates, game players move through a succession of emotions in their playing which identifies the different and enticing pleasure that games permit:

> The first time a game is played, it is experienced with a certain unfamiliarity; the world is new and salient and poses challenges and mystery. By playing the game numerous times, the game world will become increasingly familiar. The peak result of such a learning process may be a trance-like immersion in the virtual world, because of the strong neuronal links that are forged between perceptions, emotions, and actions. But the end result of the learning process is what the Russian Formalists called **automation**, and what psychologists might call **desensitization by habituation**. The virtual world becomes predictable, it loses its visual and acoustic salience and the player will probably stop playing the game at this stage. Thus, this aesthetic of repetition is based on the sequence: first **unfamiliarity and challenge**, then **mastery** and finally **automation**.
>
> (Grodal, 2003: 148)

Calling this process of involvement and mastery addiction is medicalizing what many of us do in all sorts of pursuits from gaining competence in playing a sport to understanding a subject or language. Although the compulsive behaviour may be irritating to those around who are not playing and there may be a sense of wasted time, a player is simply motivated by a desire to master the particular game in all its intricacies.

What gives electronic games an extra dimension of investment is the notion of gameplay. Gameplay has become a term used in critical reviews of particular games and has now become a way that academics are understanding the pleasures of gaming (Banks, 1998). Both simulation and first-person shooter games rely on elaborate relays of interpreting and responding quickly to conditions. It is tactile and very often filled with a tension that envelopes the body and concentrates the mind. Gameplay is how these various elements of connection to computer games intersect with navigating the rules and regulations of the game. Good gameplay implies that the aesthetics and appearance of the game align with its interactivity and the progressive level of difficulty. It is very much a feel of how the game produces itself through the player. If the player is secondary to the experience, as often happens in games derived from films, the gameplay quality is substandard.

Gameplay also implicates the kinds of narrative that are part of games. To describe games as narratives is somewhat of a stretch; but what narrative refers to in games is the general direction that they follow. In role-playing games, narrative is much more central to the experience of the game. A quality of mystery and a progressive unravelling of the enigma may be fundamental to the pleasure of the game.

Gameplay in first-person shooter games may be less about narrative than about how objectives are presented for the game and how well those objectives when reached are rewarded. Also, the perspective of first-person shooter games is critical to the operation of the game. Because the gameplayer sees only part of the body and perhaps the weapon of their character, it is important that the game maintains a coherent realism in its construction of the imaginary game space. Even failure or 'death' in games has to have a workable degradation: thus in first-person shooter games, it is common for one's 'health' to be represented by a graphic that indicates what percentage of one's powers remain. In simulation racing, as Poole explains, it is essential that crashes and bumps into the wall do not completely derail the driver: gameplay in simulation is to produce some verisimilitude but allow for its bending for the sake of the race and the gameplayer's pleasure in staying in the race (Poole, 2000: 186–7).

Gameplay also implicates how well the game holds up to repeated play. Does the game maintain its intensity for the gamer after the fifteenth play? Equally importantly, have the programmers provided enough variations, challenges and subtle extras to make the game have new elements to employ? These elements of gameplay are considerations as to how the game has embedded hidden 'cheats' that gamecoders have made possible.

Cheats are special moves related to a sequence of buttons on a joystick or console that generates something that gives the aficionado the advantage. Special magazines and websites publicize 'cheats' for games that maintain a loyalty among gameplayers resembling a secret society. Cheats also reflect a game's relationship to a dichotomy of rule structures and rule breaking that in the study of games is referred to by Callois as the open-endedness of *paidos*, or play, and the relative closed structure, *ludos* or game.

Identity and the community of gamers

There is a quality of electronic games that invites the player to cross into the screen. Martti Lahti writes about this eloquently:

> One of the characteristics of video games throughout their history has been an attempt, with the help of various technologies, to erase the boundary separating the player from the game world and to play up tactile involvement. Indeed, much of the development of video games has been driven by a desire for a corporeal immersion with technology, a will to envelop the player in technology and the environment of the game space. That development has coincided with and been supported by developments in perspective and the optical point-of-view structures of games, which have increasingly emphasized the axis of depth, luring the player into invading the world behind the computer screen.
>
> (Lahti, 2003: 159)

Lahti's argument builds on the idea that there is a corporality dimension in understanding the experience of playing electronic games. As described above, the subjectivity of the gamer is structured into a cybernetic loop so that the gamer becomes an extension of the game's directives. But what is interesting about Lahti's developed argument is how the game is a conduit for the player to move through the 'proscenium arch' of the screen. Games develop a subjectivity that, despite the deceit of the machine and software's control, is an alluring invitation to become part of an environment and to make things happen in that environment. The process of playing is a process of production. Although not a free-spirited form of production, the gamer is producing results within the ecology of the program. Like other new media, electronic games move the individual to the centre of cultural production: the gamer is the subject and the agent of the game. He or she enacts a role and makes the decisions within parameters of what that role entails. As we shall see in chapter seven, reality television also allows the individual to cross into the screen, however contrived and constructed that passage to representation might be. Games work in new media cultures as the strongest and most regular site where the individual produces their entertainment and that 30-year two-generation gamer sensibility percolates through our other media forms in interesting ways.

The cultural experience of how gamers make the game is not lost on the industry itself. Gameplayers are regularly employed to beta-test games before they move to the open market. Game testers have become an important step for the production of electronic games to eliminate glitches and to improve the connection to the core players. The integration of players into the economic structure of game manufacture also heralds shifts that are occurring in other media and in other industries. The game tester is a role that goes well beyond previous efforts to have strong feedback marketing loops with audiences. Many game testers go on to careers in the game industry based on their identification of code problems which generate the solutions to playing issues. Also, there is a large group of players who manipulate the codes of games and thereby modify a game's rules and play. Gamers who are 'mods', even though they are transforming the code of copyrighted materials are welcomed to a degree by the industry to help games morph into new editions (Marriott, 2003: E1).

Because of the array of games, there is no consistent identity or typical game player. Most games, but not all, require the player to take on an avatar as they move into the gamescape. The degree of the significance of the avatar changes with the type of game. For instance, in role-playing games, the avatar is essential and determines future alliances and progressions through the game. While in fight games such as *Tekken 4*, it is possible to choose specific characters who have special fight moves. In many games, one can choose 'to be' a male or female; however in *Tomb Raider* everyone becomes a Lara Croft in the game. In sports games built around soccer or ice hockey, the gameplayer becomes a team; in some cases part of the game is picking the team and thus the player becomes more a manager or a coach. The logic of the game is more significant around character choice than any gender-bending.

A richer area of study is the more general question of gender and gameplayers. It is widely assumed that more males play electronic games than females. In most countries this is quite accurate, although there are many female players and the male stereotype for gameplayers loses the varied nuance of gamers. According to the American Entertainment Software Association, 39 per cent of gameplayers are women (http://www.theesa.com/pressroom.html). Moreover, 57 per cent of games are bought by women. Women are also more likely to play online games and least likely to play console games than men. Although there have been efforts by educators in cooperation with key game manufacturers to make more female-friendly games (Cassell and Jenkins, 1998), there have been counter-movements to this tendency to essentialize female game pleasure. Gamegirls is one of those groups that has had a large online presence and celebrates its prowess in action and first-person shooter games. *Quake*, another first-person shooter game has had a small but visible group of female players – Quake Girls – with an associate e-zine that articulates their desire to excel on their own terms in the game. The industry itself has generally been drawn to produce the ultimate girl game or perhaps more ideally a cross-gender game. Twenty-five years ago, *Pacman* represented the game designed to attract female players. In terms of industrial strategies, perhaps movie-derived games such as *Harry Potter* might have the same cross-gender appeal.

With the average age of video or computer gameplayers in 2003 reported to be 29 in the United States (ESA, 2004), gameplayer identity and subjectivity has shifted quite dramatically over time: games have become mainstream adult entertainment as much as they are and have been part of children's culture. One of the most interesting transformations is online gameplaying, usually called multi-player online gaming (MMOG) or massive multi-player online role-playing game (MMORPG). MMOGs come in many forms and styles and originated from the multi-user domain games that resembled online *Dungeons and Dragons* games in the early decades of the internet. The simplest online games are traditional board games and are available free of charge on portals such as Yahoo! and MSNGames. Millions participate in these games and use them primarily for breaks from their everyday lives. Other games, such as first-person shooter and role-playing games, have had a more protracted development on the internet that has led to a very loyal following for particular games. One survey indicated that there were 31 million casual online game players involved primarily in traditional and simple games. In contrast, what are labelled as hard-core players numbered 8.4 million (IGDA, 2003).

As the principal software and hardware game manufacturers moved into producing online versions of their games, the number of hardcore players and quality of the multi-player games has accelerated. Three-dimensional space with multiple players, as well as many stand alone avatars created by the game are available in the most popular of the online games – *Everquest*. According to one survey, 90,000 players are logged on to the role-playing game at any one time (Armstrong, 2003). The total number of players is estimated at 2 million who roam through a virtual space of 323 square miles (Massmog, 2003). Not all games are organized for massive numbers. A trend in online games resembles chatrooms. Games between two or a group of friends are often the norm with online games. With these smaller numbers, games also betray their origins, where players once created local area networks by connecting their computers into a local network in order to play against each other. Emerging in online game spaces are similar micro-communities loosely linked to other communities. Tournaments have grown more sophisticated and professional as a more formal site for play.

Games in this online environment have become places where friendships are built and maintained through interests in particular games. Aficionados of specific games develop their own argot and acronyms that rival the best text messagers. With online games, the critique that games are socially isolating makes little sense as players build their social networks through their online game connections.

Conclusion

Through their long history, electronic games have been the most influential of new media forms in transforming the cultural landscape. Their status as divertissement perhaps allowed their influence to go unrecognized except in the most vituperous articles critiquing their debilitating effects on children. What has made electronic games particularly significant is the way that they have shifted our relationship to media and entertainment. As detailed here, electronic games were instrumental in the new blending of work and play in contemporary life. The delineations are less clear than in the past as work invades domestic space and play pervades the creativity space of the information economy. Via electronic games, the entertainment industry has also redirected itself and moved the idea of play into the structure and meaning of other forms, from film and television to popular music and radio. This shift is very much related to incorporating the essential component of electronic games and play more widely: interactivity. The kinds of engagement embodied by electronic games have become the benchmark for popular culture and presaged the prolific cultural investment and interactivity that have made the internet and the web such a fascinating and dynamic environment for information and cultural exchange since the 1990s. Games have provided for massive participation, but qualitatively different than the participation offered by television or radio. Electronic game participation implied the individual's personalization of the medium through playing the game and bringing the structure to life. I have called this a form of cultural production, albeit contained within the framework of a cybernetically interactive game. Electronic games have democratized contemporary cultural production in a patterned way: they have allowed the player to move into the action of the screen. This profound shift is a celebration of the activity of the populace to make their culture. The electronic game has been a broad channel for that will-to-produce even as it is has been brilliantly made into a successful form as a cultural commodity.

chapter six

Rejuvenation: film in the digital world

Michele Pierson makes the convincing argument that digital effects maintain a discourse of wonder for the production and reception of film (Pierson, 2002). This sense of wonder is wedded to the very illusion of cinema as an apparatus and a practice. The techniques of digital effects that we might see in the *Terminator* or the *Matrix* film series are very much a part of the tradition of film as it connects science and technology to affective moments of awe and bewilderment within film narrative. The digital from Pierson's perspective is a form of rejuvenation of the cultural form in its capacity to replay the 'shock of the new' origins of the cinema at the beginning of the twentieth century.

This chapter and the next explore the way that the now traditional media of film and television have transformed in the era of new media and digitalization. Both television and film have been very successful in the production of audiences over the last century. In the case of film, our object of study for this chapter, audiences have been drawn to its narratives and its structure of generally accessible content that can span many cultural differences through its various genres. What has been detailed in previous chapters is that the nature and status of the audience is in flux with the development of new media. Beyond the active audience, we have identified that there is a 'producerly' quality in the user of new media whether that use is via the internet or in electronic games. Similarly, the digitalization of film has presented possibilities and potentials for film to address some of these emergent democratized aspirations around cultural production. The film industry, in reaction and response to new media cultures, is developing interesting hybrid forms and patterns of production that are becoming significant components of that same culture of new media.

Film and the digital

Chapter four dealt with the constraining design structures of electronic games. In that discussion, it was possible to identify the controlling aspects that are part of game design and through that provide one counter-argument to the sense of engagement that playing games embodies. As we investigate the digital implications for film and the cultural activities that it engenders, it is useful to investigate critically film from a similar vantage point of design.

First of all, the film medium is highly structured partly because of its complex and collaborative production exigencies. As it has been industrialized, that structure has particular ends around attracting large audiences. The highly designed form of film production is related to the building of very clear narratives and, at least in its Hollywood incarnations, decisive forms of closure. These can be rethought of as aspects of the 'software' design of the film. Utilizing the metaphor of software helps us think of how film is designed to work in practice. The producers of Hollywood films are very sophisticated designers of software, who through various feedback systems, have worked out patterns that derive a certain success at providing pleasure for audiences. Hollywood, more than any other film 'system', has been able to make that software comprehensible and engaging for an array of audiences from a variety of national, racial and ethnic backgrounds. The system, as Miller *et al.* have explained, dominates the exhibition and production of film globally with the possible exception of the equally designed Indian film industry (Miller *et al.*, 2001).

In industry terms, films that are highly designed are high concept: they are driven and thereby conceptualized by a single idea that becomes the story and guiding structure for both its development and exhibition (Wyatt, 1994). What differentiates film from other kinds of computer-developed software is that its actual end use is not through the interface of the computer screen, but rather in the play of imagination and identification in the viewer. The interactivity that is so much part of the user's relationship to the web or to the playing of an electronic game through the click of the mouse or the manipulation of the joystick, is designed in film as a form of immersion in the mind itself. The screen becomes – in Christian Metz's terms – the fourth wall that opens outwards into the narrative but is designed to exert a psychological identity effect on the viewer (Metz, 1982). The viewer 'identifies' with characters as points of view, partly there to situate the action of the narrative but more importantly to 'suture' the viewer into the meaning structure of the film. The sensory quality of the darkened cinema house with the brightened fourth wall, with its characters literally larger than life, provides an 'apparatus' for the play of the imaginary that psychoanalytical film theory has likened to the dream state that underlines its psychic power in audiences. In these terms, cinema's effect is one of transference – out of the reality of the film viewer and into the reality-effect of the imaginary scenario that is presented.

Into this system of production and reception, where Hollywood has been very successful at presenting the imaginary reality-effect for the audience's pleasure for nearly a century, come the possibilities and potentials of the digital. There are four major implications that need to be developed as we think through how film as a system deals with its digital reincarnation and I will address each of these in turn.

1. **The digital presents the potential to better reconstruct the reality-effect that cinema has cultivated. Digitalization of the image permits its manipulation for even greater kinds of illusion.**

In many ways, the digital is an extension of the various illusory techniques that are part of cinema's repertoire. The digital, then, can be thought of as one of cinema's techniques of special effects which dates back to its pre-origins. Cinema's history is wedded to a number of other technologies of reproduction that were working to fabricate a virtual reality through the *trompe d'oeil*. The actual effect of film's moving image itself is one of these tricks of the eye: in reality a strip of film is a series of still images that, when projected rapidly enough in succession, produces the illusory effect, a perception of motion, because of the persistence of vision that carries the image in the brain from one still image to the next. If enough frames per second are projected the brain imagines the series as continuous motion. Cinema's standard is 24 frames per second.

The digital manipulation of the film's image makes the screen much more malleable for editors. Early digital effects were often connected to science fiction and fantasy, and were designed to make elements that could produce believability in the viewer about a certain creature or environment. For example, *The Abyss* constructed an alien figure that adopted its recognizable form through becoming more or less a tubular liquid – a pseudopod that transformed into a face. The digital effect of presenting the alien was an elaborate computer development of the image that simulated the way light would be refracted through a form that had the thick mobility of mercury but the transparency of water (Darley, 2000: 107–8). Spielberg's *Jurassic Park* fabricated dinosaurs so that their movements could be more fluid as well as provide appropriate reflection of a given environment. In a famous CGI scene, we are shown a slowly moving raptor's head with the projected computer screen image displayed over its mottled skin and yellow eyes as its searches for its next victim. These moments of finely crafted CGI were used sparingly because of the expense; nonetheless they were inserted at critical moments to heighten the believability that human actions were in the same environment as these creatures. CGI helped blend the real image with the computer-animated components.

Other films played with the capacity to manipulate existing archival film footage through inserting actors into the scenes. The film *In the Line of Fire* (1995) placed a young Clint Eastwood film image into documentary footage of the 1963 Kennedy Dallas motorcade. For both plot and character development, this fabricated past became a believable flashback to establish Eastwood's character Frank Herrigan's strong motivation to prevent a presidential assassination. Similar efforts were generated in the fantasy-historical drama *Forrest Gump*. Via digitally compositing, the image of Tom Hanks as Gump is placed into historical scenes. Also, the development of 'digital crowds' was employed in *Forrest Gump* that in effect reduced the number of extras needed for a re-enactment of a Washington Vietnam War protest.

Although clearly different uses have been made of computer imaging by the film industry, they have generally fallen into specific categories. The most common digital effect is to produce a **composite image**. In the past mattes, painting and modelling were the principal techniques used to layer an image with a different foreground or background. Much of this kind of film-making is now accomplished almost entirely through digital rendering. Thus a contemporary street can be remade digitally with vintage cars and lighting into a 1940s street scene. Likewise, transformations of skies and the composition of a city skyline can be produced more seamlessly through digital compositing. A second category is **special digital effects** that may be either too difficult or dangerous for real actors or stunt actors to complete or that are beyond the possibility of display. In the *Matrix* (1999), the slow-motion dodging of bullets by Keanu Reeves' character Neo is an elaborate effect that is dependent on digital manipulation of the image and motion and the reconstruction of an array of still cameras grabbing images around the scene. Elements of compositing are overlaid with live action and the third category of digital imaging – **digital animation**.

Digital animation currently represents the most dramatic transformation of film. In order to render simulation of real bodies in motion via computer programs and designs, digital animation demands elaborate efforts to record in three dimensions body movements for their reconstruction and simulation by computers. The first uses of digital animation appeared regularly in commercials, inserts into feature films and short films. Pixar, the most dominant producer of digital animation, produced its first complete digital animation feature, *Toy Story*, in 1995. Its box-office success ensured that other productions followed. In fact, there have been very few traditional animated features that have been successful since *Toy Story*'s release; moreover most of the 'traditional' animated films are assisted massively by computer imaging. What has emerged is a shifted aesthetic with an odd relationship to live-action features. For the audience the reality-effect of digital animation is partially determined by how close to the real the image represents or how close the film is to the cinematic-real. Thus, films such as *Toy Story* or *Shrek* (2001) produce what can only be described as an uncanny representation. They remain animation, but the organization of light and depth on objects allows for a much more three-dimensional construction of the characters in screen space. The intricate work on facial expressions and movements in *Shrek* or in *Finding Nemo* (2003) make the audience believe and disbelieve simultaneously. This sense of uncanniness, which can be thought of as the audience's uneasy relationship to the image and its perpetual state of being unsure how to categorize its qualities generically, reached its recent zenith in the film version of the video game *Final Fantasy* (2001). Here the digital animators worked at rendering what we could describe as synthespians – animated human-like figures as opposed to the stylized toys and other characters that populated most other forms of digital animation. Watching a certain character, again with the subtle facial movements as they spoke and 'emoted', blended with the actor's voice so much more completely that what is uncanny is not seeing James Wood or Donald Sutherland on-screen, but rather a model synthespian that bears no close physical relationship to these real-life actors. Perhaps this proximity with the reality-effect made it difficult to watch the film: *Final Fantasy*, for all its technical achievement, was **not** successful at the box office. Of course, the more obvious reason for its relative failure was the sheer woodenness of both the 'performances' and the actual story, which may have developed because of the overwhelming focus on the technical achievement of verisimilitude in the actors and setting. What was believed to be a natural and ready audience of game players of *Final Fantasy* did not translate into an engaged film audience.

Emerging in contemporary film via digital effects is a new form of voyeurism that needs to be explored further. Much of digital cinema is producing images that are 'real', but actually impossible to capture via conventional camera work. In this way, digital cinema is presenting a new hyperreality. The traditional horror film's play with showing the goriest parts in a series of climaxes best represents this expanded voyeurism. Digital effects promise us this extra vision into the action, from angles and situations that expand the effect and produce these similar mini-climaxes that provide a pleasure frisson for the voyeur. For instance, in *Titanic* (1997), director James Cameron's use of digital effects was to make the *Titanic* 'live' again. We see Leonardo DiCaprio's character Jack's triumphal mounting of the bow of the ship in a panoramic 270-degree tracking shot along the ship's line; the artifice of the moving ship was developed digitally as were the actual ship's deck and the people. Similarly, the scene of 'people' falling down the deck of the ship as it began to break into two and sink was produced entirely digitally. Heightened moments of hyperreal images were no doubt part of the rationale for George Lucas to digitally re-edit his *Star Wars* trilogy in the late 1990s, two decades after their original release (a more cynical view would claim, quite correctly, that it was more about guaranteed box office for a re-release). The added scenes were built as moments of this new digitally real, where the capacity of computer animation could transform the 'vision' of Lucas's *Star Wars* world more completely and accurately.

2. **New media with their forms of interactivity represent a challenge to the conventions of film 'software'. Coursing through the film industry blood lines is that its entertainment must attempt to produce the simulation of interactivity to compete with newer media forms.**

There is little question that film represents a different form of engagement than many new forms of media. There isn't the obvious connection by a perpetual human–machine interactivity. But as we have seen in cinema's digital developments, there are ways to attract the viewer and maintain an investment in the form.

In order to counteract this perceived deficiency, film has invested heavily in commentary on the cultural conditions of new media. In other words, film stories are often an engagement and debate with the effects of new media forms. In a very elaborate dialectic, the narrative around new media is both one of ostentatious display and cultural critique. The dialectic is entirely schizophrenic as film after film is a discussion of some form of technological dystopia, while there is a celebration of the employment of the technical capacities of digital production and simulation.

To get a sense of this bizarre but clearly developed dialectic, it is worth tracing its filmography. Its lineage is clearly connected to the dystopias that H.G. Wells and George Orwell penned, and film versions of this same dystopian future in Fritz Lang's *Metropolis* (1927). But in its more modern incarnations it is connected to the development of the blockbuster and its utilization of new technology for overwhelming the film viewer – what we can term an immersive aesthetic. *Westworld* (1973) and *Futureworld* (1976), two films from the 1970s, represent the beginnings of this duality as they more directly articulated the same dialectic that was embedded in Stanley Kubrick's *2001: A Space Odyssey* (1968). In these films, Yul Brynner plays a cyborg at an elaborate theme park where, as the advertisements for the film intoned, 'nothing could go wrong'. Visitors were immersed in the western via computer-controlled scenarios; unfortunately for the guests, the highly structured and cybernetic virtual environments moved from playing with life and death struggles to real hunted and hunter relationships between the robot cowboys and the theme park's guests. Interspersed with the action were images of computers and programmers working in backrooms. *Westworld* was one of the first efforts in film to present computer-generated images when the film represented how the cyborg cowboy actually perceived his universe.

The rendering resembled heat-sensitive/infrared camera images combined with an array of geometric lines and intersections, all computer generated.

Westworld represented a clear dialectic between a narrative critique of the monstrous possibilities of new media and a celebration of its capacity to transform the image into something remarkable. Disney's *Tron* (1982) followed this lineage. The storyline of *Tron* focused on providing a parallel between the evil corporate machinations of the director of a computer game company and the control of the game itself. Through some kind of transmogrification (and abduction), an actual programmer/hacker, Flynn, enters into the computer game world as a gladiator. The game is controlled by the Master Control Program; Flynn's objective is to unseat this dictator and replace it with Tron, a security program that allows users and programmers their rightful place and freedom. In dismantling the Master Control Program, Flynn is also able to unseat the corporate director in real life by revealing his past thefts of his programs. The *mise-en-scène* of the story, like *Westworld*, is designed to celebrate the magic of the computer-simulated game world. CGI helped produce various sequences and the overall look of the film, even as its contents were an expression of the threat of ultimate control that computers represented within our society.

The filmic discourse of critique and celebration of new media continued throughout the 1980s and 1990s. Films such as *Brainstorm* (1985) and *Lawnmower Man* (1992) employed various levels of computer-generated effects to reveal both the pleasures and possibilities of immersive entertainment technology; but both films diegetically exposed the dangers of losing one's identity in simulated states. In many ways, these films and the fin-de-millennium film *Strange Days* (1998) provided an odd moralistic presaging and parallel commentary on the 1990s journalistic obsession with cybersex and other internet 'addictions'. Entertainment in these new media forms went dangerously beyond fun and into something destructive in its controlling and addictive hedonism and its possibilities for different exploration. Other films, less drawn to the use of CGI but nevertheless part of the same elaborated film discourse provided further critiques of new technology. For instance, *Virtuosity* (1995) and *The Net* (1995) played with the fears around identity and security that the internet had spawned. *Hackers* (1995) romanticized the power of the sole individual to undermine the control of large corporations.

It could be argued that the *Terminator* series of films spawned the norm for blockbuster films and their schizophrenic relationship to technology. With the release of *Terminator 2: Judgment Day* (1991), it was clear that the storyline, with its future threat of machines taking over the Earth, which could only be prevented through the saving of an individual from time-travelling cyborgs was in contradistinction to the promotional campaign that celebrated the new generation of computer-generated images that the film showcased. The liquid metal morphing of the T-1000 evil cyborg became the narrative for the film's publicity campaign. The wonder of its illusion and the various explanations of how the images were produced migrated through the various talk-show appearances by the film's stars as well as being the centrepiece of the 'making of *Terminator 2*' documentary film. It is remarkable to see how the *Matrix* series of films echoes the *Terminator* series. Once again, the underlying narrative of the films is a dystopia of an entirely simulated world where humans are used merely as an energy source for a machine-dominated world. The pleasure of the film for the audience, however, is partly the way it depicts the simulated world through the illusions constructed via CGI. Like *Terminator 2*, the *Matrix*'s promotion revolved around the presentation of these remarkable special effects and a discourse around how they were achieved.

The films listed here do not represent all of the films that the Hollywood film industry has produced and the massive number of films that have employed CGI for much more routine purposes over the last quarter-century. What they do represent is how film has produced a critical commentary on new media. The way that these films have provided this commentary is to make films that fabricate the level of interactivity that is imagined for new media forms. The reality is that these new media, such as virtual-reality games or other forms of immersive entertainment, currently can not fabricate this level of interactivity. Film provides the cultural imaginary of possibility and thereby simulates for the audience the sensation of further dimensions of interactivity. The film industry's response, then, is to represent versions of the near future. Spielberg's *Minority Report* (2002) provides further examples of this capacity of a film to depict more complete levels of interactivity as it extends existing technologies. As touched on in previous chapters, we see Detective John Anderton manipulating images and information on large interconnected projected hologram screens both with his hands and via voice recognition. Later in the movie we see an imaginary future level of interactivity where via retinal recognition billboard display advertisements speak directly to Anderton inviting him to buy an array of products as he passes the images in public spaces. These possibilities are part of the current technology but clear extensions that work effortlessly in the fictional film world when freed from the more pedestrian limitations of current technology. Blockbuster films' affinity to new media is to provide a 'demo-aesthetic' of possibility and potential: fiction film can actualize the desires of current new media for the audience where the technology actually works and works powerfully.

Contained within many blockbusters is a different kind of narrative driving the action. The narrative, as Andrew Darley has explained, often has the kinetic energy of an electronic game or a theme park ride (Darley, 2000: 52–3). It is an aesthetic that does not pause except to produce moments of awe around a particular effect as it moves towards clear objectives and ends. The action film represents the fulcrum of the blockbuster in all its incarnations and stories. Film, in its effort to produce the continuous adrenaline rush for the player of a first-person shooter game, replicates the sensation via films such as *Speed* and *Speed 2* (1994 and 1997), *Twister* (1996), *True Lies* (1994), *Mission: Impossible* and *Mission: Impossible 2* (1996 and 2000) and a host of other films. The action and the causal chain leads to reaction serially until the inevitable closure. This aesthetic has developed in film in the era of new media. Coordinated with this development of action narrative, the film industry has invested in creating its own kind of immersion through IMAX film exhibition. The final part of the *Matrix* series *Matrix: Revolutions*, was simultaneously released in this large-format print (three times the size of the normal large-format 70 mm print) for massive screen presentation not only to make the film larger than life, but also to overwhelm the viewer with its imaginary representations. One can liken the current experimentation in cinema through the blockbuster in terms of narrative, technological effects and screen size as techniques that emulate the change in cinema in the 1950s with the introduction of television. In that era, film developed widescreen formats, improved sound and three-dimensional exhibitions to make film-going a more dramatic spectacle and to make television less appealing. The contemporary film industry this time around is fabricating a sensation of greater engagement and investment to match and replicate the interactive aesthetic of new media.

The continuing development and refinement of the blockbuster imperative and the expansion of digital effects represent how the mainstream film industry has responded and adjusted to the era of new media cultures. Both of these strategies are dependent on extensive capital resources and work to ensure the success of the largest of film corporations. For example, a 40-second digital sequence for the film *Titanic* cost the producers $1.1 million. Blockbusters now routinely cost in excess of $200 million. Their promotional budgets are equally massive. The strategy behind promotion is to produce complete saturation in all media forms so that the opening weekend is massive. To ensure this different form of immersion, studios now plan for simultaneous release on thousands of screens so that the maximum impact of the advertising is achieved with bums on seats within two weeks of its initial release. *The Matrix: Revolutions* (2003) expanded this strategy so that it opened simultaneously in over 50 countries, on 10,013 screens and in 43 languages, a feat never before achieved in the film industry (Holson, 2003: B1). The blockbuster is designed to create an entire media event: even local multiplexes will devote as many as seven screens showing a blockbuster round the clock in its first week of exhibition. The interactive environment of the blockbuster can be thought of as attached to a promotional aesthetic that is equal in significance with the narrative and action of the actual film; the public cannot escape knowing something about a blockbuster film because of the incredible amount of publicity and advertising that surrounds its release.

3. **The digital has reduced the costs of production and editing. Digital 'film-making' can democratize the production process and thereby open the system of film-making to new players.**

As much as this strategy represents the digital heartland of the film industry, new digital technologies allow for cheaper forms of production. One of the other principal tendencies in film production over the last 10 years has been the development of independent film both in the United States and internationally. In some instances, digital forms of production make it difficult to identify whether a given production is in fact a film. Nonetheless, what has emerged is a generation of 'films' that are nowhere near the average cost of production in Hollywood. In the United States, this has led to a new bifurcation in production of large and small budgets that makes them incomparable. Smaller films are produced for exhibition in repertory cinemas and on cable channels devoted to independent films such as the IFC and the Sundance Channel. Digital editing has provided cheaper possibilities for the completion of a project primarily because the technology of editing can be contained on a desktop computer.

There are many examples of cheaper films that have been made in the last decade to wide acclaim. Perhaps the best example of a film that embraced the ethos of new media culture was the *The Blair Witch Project* (1999). Although highly stylized, it privileged handheld camera techniques, the regular use of digital video for authenticity and the clever utilization of both single- and multi-camera digital techniques. Although the film was fictional, it was designed to appear as if the material was an incomplete video documentary that was stumbled upon and that detailed what went wrong in a college production crew's quest to uncover the mystery of Blair Witch. Drawing on what was revealed as much as what was not revealed, the film succeeded in navigating the lines of a horror film and the aesthetic of an uncut documentary.

Adding to its success, the producers worked on what could retrospectively be called viral marketing. The producers built a website for the film without revealing that the film and project were fictional. The website, filled with fragments that purportedly belonged to the missing production crew, attracted a following and connected fan websites as it moved to its first exhibition at the Sundance Film Festival, which helped maintain the ambiguity about the origins of the film in order to maintain its authenticity as a documentary. After its success at Sundance, the film was picked up for major distribution; however, the viral marketing where people found out about the film via word of mouth, was sustained, albeit with greater resources and ultimately massive distribution into the mainstream cineplexes.

It is usually distribution that connects smaller production companies to the larger film studios, and the success of independent films is crucially linked to these distribution deals. Over the last decade most of the major studios have not only trawled the independent film market at countless film festivals internationally for the next big 'independent' breakout hit, but they have also either purchased an existing independent production company or set up their own subsidiary to make their own small films. What has attracted the majors to this apparently smaller market is that the profit margins are so much better than even for the most popular blockbuster film. For instance, *The Blair Witch Project*, which cost only $45,000 to make, actually had a box office of $145 million. The major studio's commitment to the project was a $2.5 million advertising campaign and guaranteed distribution. Even counting that figure in the production costs, the profit return is 7000 per cent. If we compare this to *Titanic* with production and distribution costs of $250 million and a return of $1.3 billion, the profit return is wonderful but only five times its cost, not seventy times. Industrially, the blockbuster does return very large profits, but also represents large capital risk. If a major film studio distributes a film that has proven itself within smaller festival markets and backs it for wider release the risk capital is much smaller. As a result we have seen the emergence of a series of internationally distributed 'success' stories that have been promoted heavily by the major studios and exhibitors, and have worked aggressively at a form of viral and cult marketing. From the UK, we have had *The Full Monty* (1997) and *Billy Elliot* (2000), from the United States and Canada we have seen the emergence of *My Big Fat Greek Wedding* (2002), from Australia films such as *Priscilla: Queen of the Desert* (1994) and *Strictly Ballroom* (1992), from Taiwan and the United States *Crouching Tiger, Hidden Dragon* (2002) and from Mexico *Y tu mamá también* (2001).

Most of the independent films listed here do not necessarily depend on the cheaper production techniques that digital technology has provided; what makes these films part of this general trend is that they represent new conceptualizations of the audience and the sources of activity and production that these new formations have generated to rejuvenate the rather staid industrial forms of production and reception of the major film corporations. The film industry now resembles the music industry from the 1950s as it tries to capture trends that are developing in more localized production scenes and extrapolate them outwards to larger national and international markets. The digital 'effect' is once again similar to the transformations in production in music this time in the 1980s, where there was a proliferation in digital studios from people's basements to locations in exotic and not so exotic locales. The technology and expertise in producing a film has democratized somewhat and has become more accessible. It is important to realize that film remains an expensive and collaborative resource and because of these labour and capital needs is not as flexible a form of production as, say, producing a website. What we are witnessing in the film industry through its bifurcation is a strategy that recognizes this shifting power of the audience and the new ethos of cultural production that can be more locally developed without the loss of 'quality'.

4. **The convergence of media through digitalization presents different avenues for exhibition.**

Distribution and exhibition of film are in a state of transformation driven by the new economies of digitalization. On one level, the film industry is faced with the same threat over the control of its intellectual property that has completely unsettled the music industry. In comparison to the music industry, the film industry's difference has been its more centralized administration of distribution and, ultimately, exhibition. Films have had a very constructed pattern of release through what are called windows. For instance, for most of the last 25 years a particular film has a theatrical release window in cinema houses for one to two months, followed by its international distribution and exhibition window, followed by its release on video window, then its release on premium cable networks window and finally on national free-to-air networks window in each market. Each release window provides a different revenue stream and, cumulatively, these streams ensure the success of larger studios with connections and distribution deals with the cable and television industry nationally and internationally.

From an industry standpoint the biggest threat to structured release has been the possibility of piracy at many different points of distribution and exhibition of a particular film. Pirate copies soon circulate internationally once a film is exhibited, as digital video camera recordings or digitally copied prints of films are made quickly. Because the digital copy does not degrade in the making of copies – if the copy is well made – it is a threat to sales of the film. Copies may quickly move through some parts of the international market; but it is the internet distribution of pirate digital copies of films that threatens to transform the value of the film in some of its principal points of distribution. With the internet, the structure of controlled and centralized release of prints is shattered through its capacity to distribute/exhibit to many points simultaneously as music sites have done so successfully since the mid-1990s.

The film industry itself has tentatively embraced the digital beyond its forms of production, partly as a way to thwart this challenge to its control of distribution and exhibition. Although the technology of digital projection is now four times the price of 35-millimetre projections (Wasko, 2002: 203), the industry is moving towards a much cheaper distribution of its film masters. Ultimately, films may be sent digitally to cinema houses for projection, which would reduce the number of prints actually circulating with a film's release and operating as a major form of control (Shatkin, 2003). Simultaneous international release, as we have seen with *The Matrix: Revolutions* (2003), is aimed at a similar technique of industry regulation (Holson, 2003). Likewise massive blockbuster releases where a film is exhibited on thousands of screens simultaneously and completes its principal run within two or three weeks is another way to eliminate the success of pirate copies and to simplify the exhibition cycle through equally massive-saturation promotional campaigns. The industry has also worked on digital encryption to ensure that films cannot be copied from legitimate digital versions such as DVDs where a content scramble system (CSS) is engaged when a recording is attempted.

Beyond using legal means to curtail the theft of intellectual property, the film industry has been working actively to improve its own product by using the capacity of digitalization to create what could be described as an elaborate new intertextual commodity (Marshall, 2002). The digital versatile disc or DVD is at the centre of this strategy to provide the audience with greater and greater possibilities and connections to individual film products. The DVD, in its enormous capacity for storage, now represents one of the dominant and lucrative 'release' windows for the industry. For instance, *Spider-Man* (2001) when it was released on DVD generated sales in excess of $200 million (Audiorevolution, 2002). Contained on its two DVDs were different screen formats of the film, discussions of special effects, English, French and Spanish versions of the film, music videos associated with the film, filmographies of the principal stars, interviews with the director and the composer, an out-take reel, screen tests and two documentaries, including the HBO *Making of Spider-Man* along with a profile of the creator and other artists of Spider-Man the Marvel comic-book hero. The *Shrek* DVD in its appeal to a children's market contained a series of simple question-and-answer games about the film as well as a remarkable program that allows the user to dub in their own rendition of the dialogue over film sequences. Films surround themselves with other objects of play and promotion, which have the capacity to immerse the audience into their architecture of engagement. Many of these products and forms of entertainment are repackaged with the DVD to make a more complete film experience. Once again, the film industry is responding to the new aesthetic of engagement in formats and styles that reconstruct interactivity and audience investment through new home versions of films and a more elaborate collector-friendly version of the particular film. Whereas rental was the largest market for the movie video cassette, ownership is the objective in the construction of the DVD.

The internet and the World Wide Web have presented a further challenge to the organization of the film industry. What has transpired via the web is an interesting and often cross-purposed array of websites that cater to film. Each major film has its official website. The film industry has generally tended to use the web as an extended promotional vehicle for its primary film products. Because of the web's structure of interactivity, however, these film sites possess much more than simple promotion. *Lara Croft's Tomb Raider* provided excerpts from its musical soundtrack. Other films provide background information that resembles the material that appears later in DVD format.

Fansites intersect with these official websites in unpredictable paths that are worthy of a great deal more study in their specific attributes than can be provided here. Film fansites cluster into web rings around certain films – *Star Wars* may be the film series that has attracted the greatest amount of interest that has developed on the web. Thousands of fans have developed websites that are devoted to some aspect of the films. The official *Star Wars* site actually provides a resource centre that allows for such a community to connect to others with a similar passion for the films. It lists the 100 most successful and popular fan websites as well as providing a great number of other sources of information about past and future films. In fact, *Star Wars*' George Lucas sponsors a short film fan tribute festival and chooses the winning entrants each year for exhibition on the web (Atom Films, 2004). The web thus serves as an incredibly rich information source for the film industry; but it must be understood that the web is uncontainable in terms of what actually appears and often the kind of information may not suit the objectives of the film industry. Just as many websites of fans are supported by film studios, many others are forced to shut down for copyright infringement primarily in their use of images. The web can be thought of, then, as containing a clear tension for the film industry: it is evidently a channel to connect to and service fans; but it also represents the cultural location for what is perceived as the greatest threat to the film industry and the integrity of its product.

It is not surprising therefore that there are many sites that confront the power of Hollywood. The web provides an avenue for quite alternative forms of exhibition and distribution of film. Since the mid-1990s, there have been sites that have allowed patrons to download Hollywood films. Far more interesting are the resource sites that gather and gatekeep the production of short films. Because of the length of time required for downloading, the short film has become one of the principal web cultural forms and has been instrumental in a kind of renaissance of the genre. At Atomfilms.com, registered users can peruse categories that include action, animation and comedy. Like Atomfilms.com, ifilm also serves as a site for new independent film releases that circumvent the usual patterns of distribution and exhibition. Although these two sites represent the greatest concentration of film exhibition on the web, digitalized film/video, along with animated shorts, are ubiquitous on the internet (see Harris, 2002). The web provides something that is limited through the major film industry – a regular venue to exhibit productions that do not conform to feature-film length or theme. We can see that via the internet in this instance, film has been democratized in its distribution and because of that has stimulated a growth in production.

Conclusion

Film is now an exhibition technology that is over a century old. Its very mechanical origins with sprockets, reels, teeth and motors hark back to the inventions of the eighteenth and nineteenth centuries. Despite the rise of many other pretenders to the organization of popular culture, film as an industry and as cultural practice continues to sit atop the hierarchies of entertainment culture. What film has become in its grander theatrical exhibition is a herald. It heralds possible futures through its dialectic celebration of technology through appropriation and negation of its possibilities through Delphic dystopian narratives. Through its appropriation of digital technology, it is equipped to tell the stories of the future in a way that produces a sense of wonder. Where technology cannot quite fulfil its promise, film can pull the possible reality with digital compositing into the cinematic real of the original shot. Film is also a herald for the organization of the media economy. Through its saturation promotional campaigns, the blockbuster film enters thunderously into the collective cultural imaginary. Like a remarkable demonstration of the power of the aesthetic, film then becomes the leading edge of the intertextual commodity. Sean Cubitt writes how film's movement into the digital facilitates the transition of images into other digital forms such as electronic games: its digital animation as background helps the construction of the game itself (Cubitt, 2002: 26). *Harry Potter* or *Lord of the Rings* are well positioned for a plethora of other commodities attached to the images presented in the original films and in their digital constructions easily convertible to new games, new toys and new elements of a 'film cycle' that appear in websites and fan reconstructions of the film (Cubitt, 2002).

This rejuvenation of film is not limited to the grand-scale strategies of a lugubriously large industry. The digital has created new cultural economies. There is clearly a place for the short film via the internet. Through different websites, the digital version of film breaks down the limitations of exhibition that have controlled what it is possible for audiences to see. Digital cameras have made it possible to have filmic qualities in the smallest of productions. Although this expansive development of film is still quite circumscribed, it demonstrates how 'film' has been more accessible and is connected to the wider new media and cultural phenomenon of the will-to-produce.

chapter seven

Rejuvenation: television

Over the last 50 years television has been very successful, developing massive audiences for its content whether under the structure of national public broadcasting or commercial imperatives. The success of this model of cultural production is easy to underestimate; but to appreciate television's consistent impact it may be useful to compare audience size with that of film. One of the most successful films of all time – *Titanic* – had a US box office of $600 million. If the average ticket price were $8 that would translate to an audience of 75 million viewers over its extended run of nine months in 1997 and 1998. *M.A.S.H.*, one of the most popular television programmes of the 1970s and 1980s, achieved American television history when its final episode in 1983 was watched by more than 125 million households, which could be as many as 200 million people. The Football World Cup of 1994 achieved a worldwide audience of over 33 billion through its 52 televised games or approximately 600 million on average for each game (History of Film and Television, 2003; Internet Movie Database, 2003). It is easy to see how television can dwarf the size of audiences achieved in other media industries. There is little doubt that television has had the greatest cultural impact of any media form for the last half of the twentieth century.

Despite these overwhelming statistics about the audiences produced by television, as an industry it has been transformed and continues to be altered by technological changes. One of the principal changes has been the expansion in the number of channels delivered and available to households. Up until the 1980s, in most countries there may have been only a handful of television channels available. There were a limited number of frequencies for stations to broadcast on without some interference from another channel. This scarcity model organized television stations and severely limited the number of licences granted to companies to operate television stations. In the United States, the scarcity along with the development of affiliated networks to national broadcasters led to the emergence of the 'big three' television networks. In the United Kingdom, with even more state regulation, there were generally two or three available channels in the 1970s in most markets (the BBC and ITV). The transformation of this highly organized and centralized structure of a small number of networked stations occurred with the expansion of cable television in some parts of the world and the development of satellite-delivered television in others. Cable, in its most basic form, broke the geographical limitations of broadcasting by offering subscribers channels from more distant locations that were picked up by antenna towers and then distributed by cable to individual households. This cable system was expanded further with the development in the 1970s and 1980s of satellite-delivered stations that could be distributed via satellite receivers once again to these same cable subscriber homes. Progressively, the effect of these technologies of distribution on television was the fragmentation of the audience and a challenge to the need for centralized powerful national networks.

Throughout the 1980s and 1990s, one can see the progressive dispersion of the national audience in several directions. First of all, in countries such as the United States and Canada broadcasting no longer represented the primary means through which people received their television signals. As a result, regulations built on a broadcasting model of delivery were ceasing to serve national or even local needs and interests. Superstations or satellite-delivered channels could operate quite easily transnationally with their large footprints of coverage. Rupert Murdoch's BSkyB channel in Europe represented this shift from the national to the transnational. CanalPlus, the French-based but trans-European-distributed satellite premium channel replicated this form of delivery. In Asia, Star Channel, with its several layers of subtitles is available across Asia and South Asia. In the United States, the development of satellite stations that are also distributed by cable emerged in the 1970s with HBO and Ted Turner's WTBS superstation. This form of delivery became highly regularized by the 1980s with such mainstays of American cable television as ESPN, MTV, CNN and the Home Shopping Channel. These channels represent a second kind of dispersion: individual channels no longer needed to be an omnibus of content but could specialize in particular genres of programming. All news channels would be side-by-side with all sports channels; all movie channels would rub shoulders with all music video channels; a children's station might be next to a nature documentary channel. No individual channel would have a mission that related to the particular community or locale; rather their mission was comprehensive programming in a particular recognized genre. The range of stations would cover the array of needs of an audience – or at least that is how it was to work in theory where a true marketplace of ideas-as-programs was to flourish.

This plenitude of television has expanded further through digitalization. For the free-to-air channels, their frequencies can now be divided into a number of individual channels or converted into a few high-definition channels. In other words, they have the potential to be multi-channel platforms of content. Digitalization of cable has allowed for the expansion of possibilities for pay-per-view channels, which can now number as many as 20 or 25 distinct channels. On-demand television, where the viewer can choose what specific programs are selected and recorded for viewing from an array of premium and non-premium channels is a feature that is now being offered by American cable companies. Their advertising slogan emphasizes the sense of control that on-demand digital cable television tries to provide: 'you are the tv guide'. Through this service digital cable heralds the end of the bestselling magazine in the world – *TV Guide*. Other services have developed very successfully in European countries. The videotext information services as a television channel is relatively ubiquitous. Still other channels can serve as community access and electronically updated noticeboards of local events.

Although linking all of these trends in the development of television into one theory of change is fraught with difficulties, it is useful to conceptualize this industrial and audience migration of television as very much linked to the principal directions that have led to the proliferation of newer media forms. Television is both a precursor of new media culture and an older medium that is transforming into an interesting hybrid. As we have already detailed, new media is very much connected to the development of something beyond the active audience into various forms of cultural production. Television traditionally has represented in popular culture the most passive of pastimes and embodying this inactivity is the derogatory description of the television viewer as the couch potato. Although cultural studies approaches to television have disputed the characterization of the television audience as passive, as a cultural form it has rarely been linked to interactivity. Yet the 60-year history of television as encapsulated here is one of expansion of choices to provide different forms of engagement and investment. To many, the expansion of choice has allowed for the same kinds of content to prevail and that the presentation of channel choice actually is a myth of diversity. After all, in American television ABC is owned by Disney which in turn owns five ESPN channels, SoapNet, the Family Channel and Toon Disney, and co-owns E! Entertainment Channel, the History Channel, Arts and Entertainment Channel and Lifetime Channel. Likewise, General Electric owns or co-owns: NBC, the news channel MSNBC, the financial channel CNBC and the Bravo network. When ownership is factored into the conceptualization of choice the diversity disappears into the various media conglomerates.

Despite the overwhelming evidence of televisual monoculture, the industry has had an interesting relationship with the activity of the audience. The development of the remote control since the 1970s has to be seen as a precursor of the computer mouse and the point-and-click computer and internet world that is so celebrated for the engagement of its audience (Burnett and Marshall, 2003: 88–9). The remote control, despite the discourse of pseudo-control has periodically stood as a challenge to the economics of television. Watching television with the remote control is closer to surfing the channels than resting on an individual programme. The old economy of television depended on the viewer's resistance to changing channels – the viewer's stickiness. Programmers designed an evening of television viewing around this inertia with lead-in programmes such as the news and strong situation comedies that could support weaker comedies and dramas for the evening. Television watchers now often follow more than one programme in their active avoidance of commercial downtime. Channel surfing, as its name suggests, is closer to the activity of web surfing described in chapter four and expresses a different viewer than has been theorized when film theory has been adapted to television.

It should also be indicated that the television industry has developed the most sophisticated technology for monitoring its audience. Through Nielsen ratings, the advertisers and the networks closely gauge the predisposition of the television audience. With people meters in select households Nielsen more closely tabulates the uses of television and then extrapolates the survey into a representation of the particular national television market.

With its broadcast model, it is difficult for television to fully embrace the individualizing tendencies that seem to be an essential part of digital culture. Television historically has produced audience aggregates to sell to advertisers. By this definition it is working under a different cultural economy. To link this cultural economy more closely to economic readings, television is clearly post-Fordist in its quality of providing slight differentiations in content. Post-Fordist implies an economy that does not simply mass produce, but rather provides the possibility for variations in design for products. The car market is classically post-Fordist. The rough model of the car remains the same, but we are allowed to choose from an array of options to individualize our mass-produced choice. In cultural forms, Darley identifies the post-Fordist tendency in the development of serialization and links this to digital culture's seriating of content into many different forms and manifestations – something identified in chapter six as the new intertextual commodity (Darley, 2000: 26–9). Television has embraced this notion of differentiation within a structure of similarity in its production of serials in every genre imaginable. From a more universal perspective, the sameness of television, where channels are just variations of other channels, also presents a post-Fordist model of cultural production. Television, therefore, is a cultural industry that is transitional in its connection to the interactive audience and its new desire and will to differentiation. Through its history, television has demonstrated its capacity for developing an elaborated version of cultural production that connects to its audiences in sustained ways and that has provided a type of variety and variation in its content.

Reactionary television: responding to the increasing digital world of interaction

With new media forms invading the space and privileged position of television in the home, it is interesting to see the way that television as a very large industrial apparatus has reacted. This reaction of television can be seen in its content and in its technology. To unpack this reaction, it is important to begin with the similarities and differences between television and the computer.

Technological movements

Television, like the computer, is composed of a screen – originally a cathode-ray tube, but increasingly we are seeing versions of plasma televisions just as we are seeing flat-screen computer monitors. This connection may seem superficial; but its significance is in the electronic basis of each of these systems of display. With the electronic structure, it is possible to manipulate screen content. Both computers and televisions can divide the screen into pixels and reorientate the information that is contained in each of these pixels. What this has meant is that the production of television can divide the screen into image and graphics as we often see in newscasts or in sports programming. The television screen is highly manipulable and, increasingly, computers have been utilized to manipulate the production of the screen image. This quality of television has made it the screen precursor of the graphic interface of the personal computer. And in reaction to the graphic quality and the enormous quantity of information that the internet has provided via the computer, television has become increasingly graphics orientated. Watching any of the newscasts from Fox News to CNN, one becomes aware of the divided screen. The news ticker scrolls across the bottom as the newsreader continues on other stories at the top left. Other graphics are provided on the right third of the screen as well. On Bloomberg, other information, such as international weather, stock reports and sporting results, occupies the left third of the screen as the newsreader is positioned to the upper right in about a fifth of the entire screen. Television has worked to enrich its content to rival the flow of information that is produced via the World Wide Web. This expanded graphic quality of television is not limited to the news, but extends to placing the individual television station's logo in the corner of the screen during actual programmes. Similarly at the end of programmes, it is now normal to divide the screen with credits and a small window that advertises future programmes for the night. Digital cable and satellite services also provide a location for the expansion of information overlay on to the screen: the viewer can get background information on the programmes that they are watching. Because of television's similar technology of display, it has reacted by providing similar graphic environments to the web in its programmes.

It is important to identify one other similarity between television and the computer before we demarcate the significant differences. Like the computer, television is a transmitting technology – its content is determined by what is fed into it. Once again, this may seem straightforward, but it is easy to overlook in the celebration of new media forms. Historically television has been very successful at incorporating new uses. As we have seen with electronic games, the first versions of those games were on the television screen. Arcade games were dependent on television technology for their display. Similarly, the video cassette recorder was added on to the basic television set in the home from the late 1970s onwards. The implication of the VCR was to some degree time-switching but to a much greater degree it transformed television into an exhibition technology for films and not solely a broadcast technology. This control over exhibition was a major transformation of television use which spawned the massive video rental industry, but also allowed the relatively smooth integration of the DVD into home entertainment appliances in the late 1990s and the early twenty-first century. Augmenting the use of television even further was the development of the portable home video camera. Exhibition of home videos became a middle-class pastime from the 1980s onwards. What we can see with these developments is that television has been a technology that has adapted to provision for other technologies. These other technologies have been expressions of cultural production that are very much connected to the cultural production thesis. Television can no longer be seen simply as a technology of reception, but has integrated these elements of productive activity into its social and technological apparatus.

Where television differs from computers is in the arena of software. Television for all its add-ons of programmability, VCRs, PlayStations, and video camera display is fundamentally linear. Although the television screen can now take a computer input for display, which makes the technology simply a monitor, it is important to distinguish that the software of the computer is much more malleable in its design for use than the software for television. The origin of the software for television is generally television stations that, once again, present the linear content that it transmits. Little can easily be altered from the original transmission partly because the transmission is instantaneous. In contrast, the content of computers is actually contained on one of the drive spaces that operates as a 'memory' source. The memory quality of computers fundamentally differentiates its technology from that of television. Stored word-processing software such as Microsoft Word provides open-ended possibilities for the user to produce content. Similarly, other software programs, such as Adobe Photoshop, allow for the manipulation of images. In contrast, the television set for decades contained little or no memory. More recent versions of television sets may have contained some microchip technology that allowed storage of favourite channels, but not much else. The VCR could be thought of as a form of memory extension of the technology, but very few people have had video-editing capabilities that could manipulate content in any way that resembled computer software. Television as an apparatus – which has social, economic and technological dimensions – primarily divided its production capabilities (the television studio) from its reception capabilities (the home). Computers, on the other hand, blended these production and reception possibilities so that the personal computer in 1980 was seen as a technology of work as much as a technology of home and leisure. Television's physical location may have migrated to public spaces in airports, pubs and bars, supermarkets or waiting rooms, or occupied more rooms of the contemporary household from kitchen to bedroom, but it was rarely a technology that was embraced in the normal work environment. As an apparatus, even with its capacity to have add-on capabilities, it has remained fundamentally a technology of entertainment and connected to non-work time.

The changes in television technology can be seen as two types: techniques that have improved the quality of the image or techniques that have offered the viewer a greater sense of control. Large-screen and high-definition television are examples of television's improvement of the experience of reception through the quality of the image. In many countries, television signals are already sent out digitally and in high-definition format. The transformation of the picture quality will be instituted over the next decade both at the level of production and in the technology of the television set itself. With that improvement in picture quality, the television as a technology of transmission will rival the quality of the computer screen image.

The technology that has improved the sense of personal control of television has a long lineage, which has been outlined above. The most recent addition to the technologies of the remote control and the VCR is the personal or digital video recorder. Operating under the brand name of TiVo or ReplayTV in the United States since 1999 and 2001 in the UK, the digital video recorder is connecting the technology of the computer with the technology of the television. The actual digital video recorder (DVR) is a large hard drive that digitally records and saves the requests of the viewer for future viewing. By 2003, digital video recorders had a hard drive that could store up to 80 hours of television programming. Because of this 'memory' capacity, what I have described as the distinction between the television and the computer is partially dissolved with the DVR. The DVR as an intermediate software technology does not provide the wide functionality of computers and software, but operates in a manner that resembles the way computer technology has become an integrated element in other appliances with very specific functions and not open-ended possibilities. The specific function of the DVR is to provide an interactive and updated guide to programming choices offered by cable or satellite television. With the DVR's communication via telephone for daily updates of television schedules for the specific local area, the new technology further resembles the converged structure of the contemporary personal computer and its internet connection. In its focused functionality, the DVR provides the viewer/user with the capacity to record and collect an entire programme's series. The DVR also has the capability of having what are called 'wishlists', where the recorder searches for a particular desired movie, director or actor and, when it finds a match, records and stores it. It has an added function of anticipating and recording programmes that the viewer, given previous programming choices, would in all likelihood want to watch – a kind of Orwellian smart technology.

As Jason Mittell describes, the DVR's 'interface' – that is, the way in which the technology 'shapes our experiences with its content, setting the parameters for the user's relationship to the media as a whole' – is significant both in its relative simplicity and its transformation of how viewers use television (Mittell, 2003: 3). Mittell further explains that we have to now think of the myriad repercussions that this new interface, which is beyond the remote control and the earlier era of the channel dial, has for the institution and apparatus of television. The technology of the DVR has sold moderately in the United States. The largest DVR producer at the end of 2003 had approximately 1.3 million subscribers (TiVo, 2003). What is perhaps more significant about this technology is its progressive integration into other hardware associated with television viewing. Cable operators are developing and launching DVR/digital cable combined boxes. Computer manufacturers such as Dell and Apple have expanded the storage capacity of personal computers and provided a software connection to programme the digital recording of television. On-demand cable is operating under the same premise of the viewer/user controlling (and paying for) individual programme series and specific movies. It is also important to be aware that technologies such as TiVo have specifically been supported by the corporations who are most concerned about the control of intellectual property. While TiVo has proclaimed itself a revolution in the use of television in its promotional campaigns, with its structure of corporate control and subsidization by the major entertainment corporations it is evidently a revolution supported by the media establishment. Sony, NBC, CBS, the cable giant Comcast, America Online and Liberty Media, among a host of other corporations, are equity investors in the enterprise. The product is also twinned with major equipment manufacturers such as Toshiba, Pioneer and Sony. The DVR is very much connected to how the television industry is constituting its digital future.

The digital video recorder is placed ambiguously in its role in the television industry. On the one hand, the leading DVR, TiVo, entices viewers to eliminate commercials through pausing live television in order to accelerate through their content; while on the other hand it is encouraging advertisers to invest in commercials that are housed on the playlist of TiVo itself. With advertising the economic driving force of the industry, TiVo is developing a different model for television. TiVo calls its advertising 'embedded commerce' (Boddy, 2002: 250) and encourages a new relationship between advertisers and their potential audiences. Long-form and explanatory ads are encouraged under TiVo. Certain major corporations have experimented with TiVo's means of connecting to an audience. Films and music are given 'profile' advertising support around their release dates. Car companies, such as BMW, can explain in great detail the advantages of their luxury cars.

Content transformations

In the digital transformation of television, the DVR does represent one very possible future. The pattern of a short series of commercials interspersed with programme content may in fact be in decline as the business model for television. Connected to this development is the remarkable success in the United States of premium subscriber channels such as HBO and to a lesser degree Showtime. Several HBO series, including *The Sopranos*, *Six Feet Under* and *Sex and the City*, rival audience figures achieved on the major commercial networks despite having a potential audience base of less than a fifth of the major networks. Indeed, the finale of *The Sopranos* in December 2002 had 12.5 million viewers (Keller, 2002) while its season premiere in September 2002 had an audience of 13.5 million. *Six Feet Under* has audiences around 5 and 6 million. *Sex and the City* also has a large and loyal audience, which has encouraged networks to bid on its syndication rights.

The traditional free-to-air networks are also in decline and causing the advertising world of television to change. In the United States, although the number of recognized networks that have stations that operate beyond cable and satellite has increased to six, the total percentage of the audience watching network television is now about 48 per cent, a steady fall over the last 15 years. In the week 7–13 April 2003, no network had an audience greater than 13 per cent or an 11.5 share of the audience (CBS). In the 1970s a top programme would have a 30 per cent share of the available audience. This pattern was maintained for most of the 2002–03 season. With the dispersion of the audience across the cable and satellite universe, along with the expansion in the use of DVR technology, there is a bifurcation in television. Audiences are moving closer to direct allegiance with particular programmes and not watching an evening of television. What has been labelled the 'hammock' programme, a weaker series that is placed between two stronger programmes, is just not as workable as it once was. Although skewed to a richer demographic, the premium channels are forming an audience cluster that actively avoids commercials in its following of discrete programmes. On the other side of the divide is commercial television, frantically reorientating its content into some new way to attract its dwindling and less-demographically-appealing-to-advertisers audience.

With the whole nature of programme flow under threat from the audience and with audiences seeking different sources for information, television in the era of new media is serving a shifted function. Network news is in steep decline – it no longer fulfils its role as the beginning of an evening's viewing. The industry has responded by producing programmes that reconstruct in serial form event television. Event television identifies the moments when television moves to a primacy of place in how people interpret world events. Large sporting events such as the Olympics and the Football World Cup operate as event television. Likewise, a national crisis such as the 2003 Iraq War or even the weeks following 11 September 2001 produced event television where people turned to television first to interpret and process the images of a particularly traumatic international news story. For the television networks, events can rarely maintain audiences and by their very nature they are relative unique occurrences. The international television industry has recently developed new generic types of programmes that try to capture this feeling of event television. And as Albert Moran has developed, these trends in television are replicated quite rapidly in multiple international markets; copycat television, where program types are syndicated for different national audiences, has become the industrial norm (Moran, 1998). Television networks in Australia, in Britain and in the United States are serializing and 'stripping' these manufactured event television structures in order to attract loyal and returning audiences. Copycat syndicated television at one time operated at the level of the lower end of television production – game shows and soap operas were the models that were exported from one market to another. The difference in a much more dispersed audience era is that these genres of games have been hyped for network prime time to become events. They have replaced the 1980s favoured strategy of the major mini-series as a genre that is designed to invade the everyday lives of a national audience to engage with a particular television programme.

The response of the television industry has even been more sophisticated than simply manufacturing regular events. In a much wider linked phenomenon, television has also developed programming types that celebrate audience involvement and investment. The traditional game show has always iconically embodied the audience in its format – contestants for game shows are chosen from loyal viewers who understand the game and play it at home before they appear on the programme. Television's attempt to intersect with new media culture and its transformed audience of 'users' and 'produsers', has led to the pervasive incorporation of the audience into television formats. Reality television is one of these genres and along with lifestyle programmes expresses television's response to new media culture both in its attendant level of interaction and its tendency to be dispersed across new and more traditional media for various uses.

The origins of this trend can be seen emerging from newer cable television channels. The all-music channel MTV since the early 1990s had diversified into representing an array of youth cultural activities (Williams, 2002). Instead of simply music videos, the channel began developing programmes that involved showing their audience in different settings. The series *Real World* began in 1992 and was the simple idea of placing seven twentysomethings together in a shared house. Their exploits were then edited into half-hour episodes. Contemporaneous with *Real World* were the various game shows that engaged the audience in gender-style battles and the spring break specials. *Road Rules*, which began in 1994, took the concept into a travelling motorhome and a game quality as college-aged students toured specific countries with specific missions.

Child-orientated channels developed parallel strategies of building loyalties to their audiences. By the late 1990s, Nickelodeon was broadcasting programmes that matched more closely the rhythm of life of school-age children. Live programming, beyond animation, with live audiences, such as *Super-slime Live*, built a closer connection to their core demographic. 'Nick invades your school' was another successful formula for making the audience part of the programming in a way that hadn't been fostered in Children's television since the 1950s.

With Nickelodeon, club-like television with antecedents back to *The Mickey Mouse Club*, resurfaced in the 1990s.

The emergence of this trend in television in the mid-1990s was very much linked to the expansion of the World Wide Web and a different new media audience-sensibility. It is also significant that the trend towards engaging with the audience more directly was initiated with youth television where reading of that new sensibility was first registered in the television industry. MTV and Nickelodeon quickly developed very elaborate websites that further connected to their audiences, providing powerful feedback loops for their own future programming strategies. Nickelodeon now divides its website between pre-school and school-age sites. Simple games are provided on the site that provide ways for children to further engage with their animated favourites. MTV has one of the most sophisticated television websites: with music news and a coordinated message board, background details about current programmes, and other related videos and information, MTV.com establishes a strong internet presence that acknowledges how much the web is a source of news in and around youth-related activities.

The web–television nexus has strengthened over the last decade. In dramatic programming the greatest experimentation has once again been in programmes aimed at younger demographics. *Dawson's Creek* developed a standalone website for the WB Network programme that allowed fans to see the lead character's computer desktop. Fans were encouraged to register and receive email updates on the programme's content. The designer of the site, Christopher Pike of Sony Pictures Digital, saw its principal objective as providing a fan's bridge for the seven-day gap between episodes. This was expanded further to keep fans engaged with the exploits of the characters over the summer hiatus when only reruns were programmed on American television (Burnett and Marshall, 2003: 92). Soap operas have also been a point for internet expansion and proliferation of related fan websites (Baym, 2000). What emerges is the building of audience loyalty by providing greater details and behind-the-scenes information for the more committed viewer. Television has used the web to build a form of brand loyalty for its programmes and there is little doubt that some of the greatest traffic on the web is to television-related sites.

From the late 1990s, the 'cannibalization' of the audience by television – where the audience is the subject of television programmes – has continued and intensified. Reality and lifestyle programmes are as much part of smaller cable channels as they are now elemental to major networks. Although not reality television, but expanded game shows that became event television, *Who Wants to be a Millionaire?* and *The Weakest Link* created an international phenomenon for major networks in drawing the viewer back to network television for as many as four nights in succession. The size of the potential prize, a million dollars, provided the allure for the game show that transformed these trivia programmes into events. Competitions such as *American Idol* or *Popstars* or other international variations also franchised successfully in national markets. The audience involvement was further expanded: audiences voted on which performers advanced to next week's programme until one was left standing. In the 2003 *American Idol* series, the votes for the finalists rivalled national elections: 24 million votes were cast on websites, by phone or through text messaging with Reuben Stoddard winning by 130,000 votes (BBC News, 2003).

By 2003 reality game shows had become the industry standard for programming. Following the success of the original *Survivor* (2000) and its incarnations before and after in various formats, the blending of ordinary people placed in extraordinary circumstances with multiple cameras recording their every movement became industrially produced by television internationally. The list of reality-based game shows is extensive: *Big Brother* (a game show version of *Real World* that has been enormously popular in the UK and Australia), *Joe Millionaire*, *Temptation Island*, *Fear Factor*, *Meet the Parents*, *Bachelor*, *Bachelorette*, *Race around the World*, *Love or Money*, and so on. With only a few exceptions, the contestants are generally in their twenties. What becomes evident is that the television industry is working on an elaborate strategy to recapture the interest of youth.

Another range of programmes can be classified as lifestyle programmes that have also been linked with the game show genre and thereby lay claim to a similar status of reconnecting and representing their own audiences. Emerging from gardening, home repair, beauty advertorials and cooking shows, this new generation of programmes deals specifically with personal and property transformation. *Trading Places*, the Australian *Auction*, the British and Australian *Changing Rooms* and *Ground Force*, the American *Dream Home* shift the demographic to the propertied middle class. Viewers are invited to watch couples with expert help transform their homes or rooms. *Auction* deals with the various parties interested in buying a house before its public auction and through its camerawork and voice-over quickly moves towards the melodramatic. Other programmes such as *Queer Eye for the Straight Guy* or the British and American versions of *Trading Places* work at personal transformations that are very much connected to the exigencies of contemporary consumer culture. More dramatic in their transformation are programmes such as *Extreme Makeover* (US, ABC Network), which have documented cosmetic surgery operations for individuals; participants receive free plastic surgery in exchange for allowing cameras to cover their every move and thought leading up to the surgery, the surgery itself and the final unveiling in front of friends and family.

A final cluster of programmes that are connected to the reality television genre are the celebrity programmes. MTV's *Cribs* is a series that tries to reveal the everyday and somewhat mundane lives of pop stars. Drawing on *Lifestyles of the Rich and Famous*, *Cribs* updates the style by making the celebrity's lives resemble that of the great number of reality television programmes that surround their exploits. *The Osbournes* (MTV, 2002, 2003) has attempted to present the bizarre 'family' life of heavy rocker Ozzy Osbourne. In synergy with the genre, the programme is presented in classic fly-on-the-wall quality and stripped down to show the almost incomprehensible Ozzy, his wife, and his teenage son and daughter dealing with living in their mansion in Los Angeles. In a similar vein, *The Anna Nicole Show* (E!, 2002–03) presents the former porn star and widow of an octagenarian Texan millionaire transform her life to fit into the scene in Los Angeles. *The Anna Nicole Show*'s claim to fame is the banality of her life, which is presented with some irony by the editing of the basic documentary-style camera work and with some subtitles. By late 2003, Fox had launched a reality quasi-celebrity programme called *The Simple Life*, which chronicled the life of hotel heiress Paris Hilton and Nicole Richie, the daughter of Lionel Richie, living with a family in rural Arkansas. Designed to be both humorous and kitsch, Fox's *The Simple Life* mixed the fabrication of wealth with poverty for effect.

The sheer number of reality television programmes that have been produced in the last five years is truly astounding and has gone well beyond the number that have been listed in this chapter. The genre has rocked the Hollywood television writing communities as networks have developed fewer comedies and dramas in favour of trialling the comparatively inexpensive reality television programmes. Although there are many insights that can be drawn about the phenomenon of reality television and there have now been a number of good critical investigations of the form (see, for example, Dovey, 2000; Andrejevic, 2003; Brenton and Cohen, 2003; Murray and Ouellette, 2004) one element can loosely group the initiative. Television is trying to rejuvenate itself. Reality television is the current path towards positioning television in the new constellations of entertainment in the digital era. We can isolate here some of the features of reality television that intersect with the new exigencies of interactive forms of entertainment.

1. **Reinvigorating the role of the audience: a televisual form of interactivity**
   Reality television reinvigorates the role of the audience. From recruiting its 'actors' from its audience and allowing the audience to determine who is voted off a programme to the documentary style of celebrating the everydayness with the extraordinary, reality television gives television the gloss of connecting to its audience more strongly than through dramatic programming. In conjunction with websites and internet chatrooms, the television industry has used reality television to become an interactive form.

2. **The immersive quality in production and reception**
   Reality television has an immersive quality. In terms of the production technique of cameras everywhere, reality television tries to construct a narrative but maintain a sensation that what is presented is unedited. In their use of documentary effects, with mini-cameras and handheld shots interspersed with 'hidden' webcam voyeuristic shots, reality programmes work to reconstruct the feel and experience of the given setting. With their website homes, the audience can invest more fully in the various directions of a particular programme's players. The game quality also attaches the programme to, however obliquely, an aesthetic of electronic games. What is cultivated is a sensation of audience commitment through a more complete sensorium of the programme. With their often stereotypical participants, reality programmes' closest new media relative is the electronic god-game *The Sims*, where the gameplayer controls the actions of various individuals and families. Reality television games are the televisual versions of these god-games, where both the audience and the game-master become part of the controlling elements of the interactive game.

3. **The flattening of participation and value**
   One of the fundamental features of the internet and the web is the lack of gatekeeping around who can participate. Thus, as discussed in chapter four, websites may arise from institutions as much as individuals. Homepages may be those officially developed by a particular celebrity or they may be shrines developed by the most avid fan. With the

quality of websites, it is difficult to distinguish the home-produced site from those derived from more official and costly origins. Reality television is the television industry's response to this levelling of participation. If we think of television as the apparatus that has bestowed significance on events and people for the last 50 years, this particular moment describes how television is actively manufacturing its 'celebrities' – its significant people – from its audience. Even within the reality television genre, there is the intersection of the celebrity reality shows with the 'contestant' shows. The distinctions and differentiations cannot be so clearly seen. Winners of game shows – except those from the 1950s – have rarely been celebrated, discussed and gossiped about in the way that reality show winners and losers move from their own programmes into specials, news programmes and talk shows, as well as on to newspaper and magazine covers. This circulation of reality programme participants into the rarefied world of entertainment celebrities is indicative of how television has made a mythic representation through reality television of its audience.

4. **Exhibiting in representational form the cultural production thesis**
   For the television industry, reality television programming is still all about constructing audiences. Most of these programmes, with very few exceptions, are designed for commercial advertising-supported networks. Yet the nature of these programs highlights a central dimension of new media culture: the will-to-produce. The various reality programmes that deal with lifestyle changes and home improvement are exemplary of this desire to produce and they represent television's technique of conveying this new wider subjectivity. Other reality television programmes, by virtue of the game quality celebrated and the use of audience as participants in the game, are also providing an exhibition of cultural production.

Conclusion

Television, as a cultural institution and as an industry, carries a great deal of baggage as it transforms into a new media form. It has been a broadcasting technology and has developed expectations around what and how it re-presents our world. Those patterns of representation are currently in flux. What we are witnessing through television is a rejuvenated form that is still very reliant on its principal objective of manufacturing audiences, but realizing and working to produce programmes and content that lead to greater investments and engagements by audiences. Purely as a technology, television has expanded outwards beyond its historical role as a broadcaster through its related new media extensions such as videogames, VCRs, DVRs and DVDs. Each of these technologies has highlighted a sense of control by the user. Similarly, with the dispersion of audiences not only to many more television channels but also to different new media forms and technologies, television has invested in genres like reality television, which enliven the institution of television with a sense of greater audience participation and investment. At this particular cultural moment, it is unclear whether television will consolidate as a technology that provides distinctive narratively driven fictions and non-fictions and maintains an appliance-like functionality in providing these kinds of programmes or whether it will mutate or converge with the technology of the computer and the internet and attempt to provide much more interaction. What is clear is that the economy of television is transforming specifically because of new media culture and the different user sensibility that has become normalized in contemporary culture.

Conclusion: the indiscretions of new media

It is often easy to assess the current array of media as just extrapolations of what has already developed. Political-economic analysis rightly points to the continued and increasing concentration of media ownership. Five recording companies, themselves part of larger conglomerates, control the production of popular music. Rupert Murdoch's News Corporation still expands its influence through the acquisition of satellite services, satellite channels and an array of cable-delivered television superstations beamed to all continents on the planet. The internet, for all its diversity, still has allowed for the emergence of these same large corporations to become the most popular websites. Indeed, when there is any successful web-based start-up company, the major media players are usually some of the key investors. TiVo, as we have seen was supported by a consortium of major existing entertainment corporations. The blockbuster film, as discussed in chapter six, is clearly a strategy that is connected to maintaining an industrial hegemony for the leading film studios and production companies.

This book has charted a somewhat different course while acknowledging these significant forces of maintaining the centres of cultural power. The newness of new media has to be seen as a cultural challenge that as much as it reveals the efforts of industrial consolidation and transnational global strategizing, also betrays its opposite. The new of new media represents the elixir of cultural change and transformation, and the uncontainability of these strategies. These new cultural apparatuses of connection and cultural exchange need to be understood as a transforming echo with the populace and forms of popularity that often herald larger transformations in contemporary culture.

I have developed a reading of new media that moves beyond the inceptions of a given technology and ponders the manner in which it is being deployed and used. Technology can never be thought of as separated from its use; and use has the capacity to transform products. Thus, new technologies, which may have been designed with particular commercial ends in mind, must be seen as revolutionary not simply in their design, but in their redesign by people. Within the design of many new media technologies is a utopian conception of change in use. The utopian quality ignites the cultural imagination of users and draws people to the newness of any particular technological gadget. In this study of new media cultures, we have worked both to identify the cultural imaginary that has been fostered by a new technology that engages users and to trace how that pleasure and desire has altered the original meaning of the form.

At the heart of this investigation of the newness of new media has been an attempt to refocus the way that cultural studies analyses media. We can think of the first half-century of cultural studies, since its emergence with the work of Raymond Williams (1958) and Richard Hoggart (1957), and its expansion outwards internationally from Birmingham from the 1970s, as a wonderfully rich exploration of cultural reception. As detailed in the first chapter, cultural studies developed a corpus of work that investigated the activity of making sense from the available artefacts and then making them meaningful within particular cultural contexts. It was an intellectual and political project that was working against the grain of the accepted definitions of culture and the selective tradition of particular national cultures. Privileged in media and cultural studies was the audience, which was thought of as active and engaged as opposed to passive and manipulated. The political and cultural project of cultural studies was aligned with understanding cultural practices from those not constructing the ideology of a nation, but rather those that had to live and make do within that culture.

New media do not miraculously change this constellation of power and resistance that cultural studies has chronicled in all its subcultural manifestations and moments. The terrain of popular culture remains, as Stuart Hall intoned almost a quarter-century ago, a site for contestation and struggle over meaning (Hall, 1981: 228); however, the way that popular culture is made and enjoyed through the forms of new media has shifted and this demands a similar movement in how we analyse this cultural terrain. To use Raymond Williams' terminology, there is a different 'structure of feeling' (Williams, 1965: 64–88) in contemporary culture because the cultures of new media have to a degree broken down the dialectical dichotomy of production and consumption or, in communication terms, the hierarchical structure of senders and receivers.

From both directions, we have explored this disintegration of the dichotomy that has more or less been a given in media production for most of the twentieth century. The social category of the audience is not so prominent in the era of new media cultures. As we have explored, it is more accurate to speak of users or gamers or by some other name that identifies the activity of the former 'audience'. Even in forms such as television and film where the audience as social construct still makes sense, there is a fraying at the edges of what that definition now means. Part of the process of new media cultures is an incredible movement towards the personalization of media so that the collective notion of the audience has less salience. The one-on-one relationship to the cultural form of digital television and more clearly with the internet or electronic games creates a heightened sense of agency in the user. Simultaneous to this growing personalization of media with MP3 players and mobile phones, is a stronger notion of connectivity in new media. Our exploration of this connected 'structure of feeling' is not as massive audiences, but rather as new networked communities that can maintain contact through several methods. Emerging from this highly wired and wireless population are also new cultural politics and distinctive ways to invest more heavily in a given array of interests.

Production as a category in what Paul du Gay *et al.* have called the 'circuit of culture' (1997) has likewise been undermined from several directions. The level of interactivity that has become part of the technological design of new media forms has blurred the distinction of where the product ends and reception begins. In electronic games, the player becomes part of the game as an agent. As one game genre's description – first-person shooter – underlines, there is a direct link between the game and the gamer. In role-playing games, the sublimation of the individual into the character goes well beyond what may occur in the audience watching television. Through the internet, websites are not the sole province of the media industry: there is a cacophony of producers that vie for our eyes and allow us access to private worlds and new constellations of information. Millions of those websites produced have no clear commercial intent. Even television, the stalwart of old media, and its relation to audiences, has transformed in an embracing dance with its audience as content through reality and lifestyle programmes as it relies more heavily on representations of its audience members' lives. Through digital video and the possibilities of the web as showcase, there is a visible tremor in the film industry's elaborate filtering devices for controlling the means of production, distribution and exhibition.

Central to all these transformations around production is the nature of the contemporary cultural commodity. In the twentieth century, the culture industries have had reasonable success at making the cultural commodity discrete. What I am implying by the term 'discrete' is the high level of control of the cultural object and limited access to it either physically or materially by its audience of users. For instance, for a film-lover to see a particular film in the 1950s or 1960s, would have to wait for its exhibition at a theatre or its transmission on a very limited range of television channels. There was industrial control through limited rental of the number of prints of the film. Similar techniques of control were evident in popular music. What was unpredictable and 'indiscrete' was the cultural imaginary of the audience and what kinds of meanings, experiences and new directions may have been spawned from the film or other cultural commodity. This study of the remaking of meaning was one of the principal intellectual projects of cultural studies: for instance, how popular music worked to transform British youth in the 1950s and 1960s.

Throughout the latter part of the twentieth century, the culture industries were quite successful at maintaining methods for making the discrete cultural commodity. For instance the CD produced enormous profits for the recording industry in the 1980s and 1990s as it maintained the purchase of the musical cultural product and stimulated a new generation of music collecting. Likewise, film has been able to maintain the discrete film commodity through its continued system of seriated windows of exhibition via theatres, video/DVD rentals, premium cable, and wider television release. With the development of audio and video cassette recording, there has always been some breakdown in the control of the cultural commodity; pirate cassette tapes of popular music and film were part of developing countries' marketplaces from the 1970s onwards and represented the marginal breakdown of the economy of cultural production.

What defines new media cultures is the wider emergence of the **indiscrete cultural commodity**, where challenging the hegemony of production was no longer a marginal activity but was occurring in the affluent economic heartland of western Europe, North

America, Australia and bands of the middle classes throughout Latin America and Asia. As diverse cultural forms became digitalized, it became increasingly difficult to control the parameters of its commodity status. The process of digitalization made production as virtual and ethereal as the light and sound of a film, as potentially uncontrollable as the cultural imaginary that had been nourished by the cultural industries for most of the previous century with enormous industry profits.

The indiscrete cultural commodity, through its own digital code, is a place for the appropriation and utilization of elements of that code for different purposes and different ends. The digital copy is identical to its original and bears none of the stigma that previous-era copies possessed. Thus through music file sharing and code manipulation, new versions of recordings emerged for swapping via the internet. The control of the original – even the idea of the original – made less sense. Moreover, the discrete commodity represented by the CD is being transplanted by either self-burned CDs or, more widely, the collection and cataloguing of hundreds of musical selections that bear little connection to the original way that the industry had marketed the music as a distinct material object. In 2004, the selling of the *Grey Album*, DJ Dangermouse's mix of the a cappella rap of Jay-Z's *The Black Album* with The Beatles' melodies and rhythms from their *White Album* to create a compelling new sound, provoked the ire of EMI, the copyright owner of The Beatles' music (Schachtman, 14 February, 2004). In a similar vein, remixes of songs by individuals made available for downloading make the formerly discrete song mutable and malleable as its digital codes are shifted, transformed and remade.

Music represents the most obvious version of the operation of the indiscrete commodity where the commodity bleeds into other actions and other forms of production that are not necessarily driven by their commodity status; but it is also a fundamental feature of the web and the development of websites. The html codes and javascript, the basic building blocks of web pages, can be copied for the purposes of making something new and different. The movement of images and designs around the web for particular, often idiosyncratic, uses is commonplace – so ordinary that it rarely becomes thought of as theft. The Open Source movement, which encourages the sharing of developed codes of programs so that new software can develop and innovations can be advanced without proprietarial restrictions of copyright, further breaks down the discrete cultural commodity.

Nick Dyer-Witheford develops an intriguing metaphor that helps us understand both the indiscrete cultural commodity and the new versions of cultural struggle that are part of new media. He links the historical enclosure of the English commons beginning in the late Middle Ages to the enclosure of the 'digital commons' by commercial and government fiat in the late twentieth and early twenty-first century:

> Villagers lost access to grazing, fishing, hunting, quarrying, fuel, building materials, and rights of way. An entire culture based on shared usage was annihilated and replaced by a new economy in which landlords developed estates as capitalist enterprises, selling the outputs as commodities on a growing world market … The evicted rural populations became paupers, vagabonds, and beggars, migrated across the oceans, resorted to soldiering,

sailoring, or prostitution in the city, or eventually were compelled to work for a wage in the new 'manufactories' – thus providing the first proletariat for industrial capitalism.

(Dyer-Witheford, 2002: 130)

The dramatic change in a way of life for 'commoners' did not occur without a struggle. There were many efforts to counter the closing common land and even stronger drives to suppress the insurgents, described by the 'rulers of the day ... as a many-headed "hydra" whose regenerative powers resisted their own "Herculean" attempts at decapitation' (2002: 131). Dyer-Witheford sees a similar struggle over the commons of the internet as commercial forms encroach on claiming virtual property in cyberculture and as governments actively encourage this transformation of the internet. In various guises, from hackers to pirates, from Open Source advocates to anti-globalization 'hactivists', a similar contestation over the commons and definition of public wealth is occurring. What Dyer-Witheford finds interesting is the new kinds of resistance appearing and growing – like new heads of the hydra – from the new connections that have been provided by the internet itself (2002: 132–56).

The cultural study of new media is working out this fundamentally different but parallel terrain of the 'digital commons'. The indiscrete cultural commodity that unravels through the uses made of its form is at the core of understanding both the terrain in which commercial entities try to make the cultural industry work and generate revenue, and the new productive subjectivity of the new media user that challenges the cultural industry economy in multifarious ways.

Here is the key shift in media and cultural studies: Fiske's resonating description of the contemporary cultural condition, which can be summarized in the rich expression 'the art of making do', needs to be amended into a cultural struggle over the 'art of making' in new media. 'The art of making' has elements of a dialectical tension as well as components that imply the becoming quality of the machinic assemblage and rhizomes that Deleuze and Guattari have posed to understand connections and temporary formations within culture.

Commercial new media forms now attempt to cater to or incorporate the 'art of making'. The most successful formation of this is the electronic game. In their sophisticated designs they provide an elaborate ecology of interaction for the player to produce themselves, and to make and remake the game with each successive start. By fabricating an environment of choice where the player makes the decisions and becomes the avatar, the game creates a sensation of producing the virtual self. It is no wonder that this highly designed cultural form has moved to the centre of the entertainment industry: its designed indiscreteness has been embraced by millions of players.

On a lesser scale, karaoke and the New York club trend of Movieoke are hybrid structures that move the cultural commodity into a realm of the art of making. The cultural commodity with karaoke becomes indiscrete in its invitation for the individual to complete the song through singing where the melody and lyrics are recombined. As detailed in chapter seven, reality television is an industrialized and highly constructed version of the indiscrete commodity in its appeal to its audience to make the programme.

The very success of these new media forms is undermined by the reason for their success.

Production becomes a combinatory and hybrid process that awkwardly invites the user to complete the commodity. Mods, as discussed in chapter five, modify games for their own purposes: they change characters and settings, and work on transforming some of the objectives of games. Although the game industry has warily accepted some of these developments by users, it is painfully aware of how these transformations threaten the sanctity of its intellectual property rights. The internet has defied many of the efforts towards commodification precisely because of its inherent indiscrete networking of information flows. What we see in the internet is millions of websites that are disconnected from commercial intent, but networked into the new flows of information and cultural activity for different communities of users. The excessive quantity of websites has actually made the commercial rationalization of the web – what Dyer-Witheford (2002) calls digital enclosure – more difficult to achieve. Perhaps where we see the greatest commercial success is oddly where commercial entities have given significant elements of access free of charge. Email and internet relay chat are offered free by Yahoo! and msn and we have further examples of the indiscrete new media commodity: once again one can see that the content of these forms is produced by the users themselves through their conversations and networking. The economic value of this massive aggregate of users is linked to their making use of the channels of communication.

Other economies develop from this connection and interaction between the user and digital forms, the very porousness of the forms allowing new media to absorb new information. In other words, information is regularly generated in new media cultures about the user. That information is sold and circulates rapidly through the culture to target more precisely the intersections between our desires and new commodities. This cybernetic 'circuit of culture' runs parallel and feeds from the will-to-produce that defines contemporary cultural experience.

The political, cultural and intellectual project of media and cultural studies in the era of new media needs a shifted sensibility to read what Johan Fornas *et al.* described as the 'digital borderlands': the categories of forms are in flux as much as the way that old and new forms are used (Fornas *et al.*, 2002: 1–41). I have argued that understanding cultural production is essential for getting closer to the different tensions and struggles that are part of new media cultures. For instance, the producing self of new media is an exposed identity that moves us to think further about the private and the public in an era of pervasive 'making' and endless becoming. Similarly, much more study needs to be developed that looks at the intersection among work, non-work and the complex activity of play. It is at this intersection that we can understand better the different meanings and discourses that can be attached to the concept of production.

Two other borders that have had years of study need to be reinvigorated as loci of analysis and inquiry in the era of new media cultures. First, further work about technology and subjectivity needs to be developed that is able to examine interactivity and the human–machine interface, and that can address the tensions between a cybernetic explanation that emphasizes surveillance, control and systems, and a cultural study of empowerment, investment and positivities of technological synergy and extensions of the self or the community. Finally, the commodity needs to be reinvestigated both in terms of its cultural value and its new configuration in enveloping new patterns of cultural production by users. In its new media status, the cultural commodity is remarkably indiscrete and porous to intervention, mutation and transformation. New media forms and the pattern in which they have been used have made it clear that one of the cultural struggles is over the boundaries of intellectual property.

New media cultures, with their many particular communities and transformed networks of connection, present a clear challenge to our skills of analysis. An understanding of a new cultural sensibility around cultural production and cultural reception is required to decipher the new media cultures. This book is intended to begin that journey of investigation and intervention.

Bibliography

Arspeth, Espen J., 1997: *Cybertext – Perspectives on Ergodic Literature*. London: Johns Hopkins.

Allan, S. and Zelizer, B. (eds) 2002: *Journalism after September 11*. London/New York: Routledge.

Anderson, C. and Dill, K.E., 2000: 'Videogames and aggressive thoughts, feelings and behavior in the laboratory and in life', *Journal of Personality and Social Psychology* 78:4, 772–90.

Andrejevic, M., 2003: *The Work of Being Watched*. Rowman & Littlefield.

Ang, I., 1991: *Desperately Seeking the Audience*. London: Routledge.

Armstrong, E., 2003: 'Fellowship of the onling gamers', *Christian Science Monitor*, 15 July, online: www.csmonitor.com/2003/0715/p13s02-lecs.html.

Arnold, M., 1994: *Culture and Anarchy*. New Haven, Ct: Yale University Press.

Atom Films, 2004: 'The Official Star Wars Fan Film Awards', online: http://atomfilms.shockwave.com/af/spotlight/collections/starwars/.

Banks, J., 1998: 'Controlling gameplay', *M/C – A Journal of Media and Culture*, www.media-culture.org.au/9812/game.html.

Barlow, J.P., 1993: 'Putting old wine into new bottles: the economy of ideas', *Wired* 2:5, 1.

Barthes, R., 1972: *Mythologies*. Annette Lavers (trans.). New York: Hill and Wang.

Baudrillard, J., 1983: *Simulations*. Foss, P., Patton, P. and Beitchman, P. (trans.). New York: Semiotext(e).

Baudrillard, J., 1991: *The Gulf War did not Take Place*. Sydney: Power Publications.

Baym, N.K., 2000: *Tune In, Log On: Soaps, Fandom and Online Community*. Thousand Oaks, Ca: Sage.

BBC News, 2003: 'Idol final attracts 38 million', 23 May, on line: http://news.bbc.co.uk/1/hi/entertainment/tv_and_radio/2933408.stm.

Bernstein, D., 2003: 'Making something out of nothing', *New York Times*, 18 December, E1, 6.

Bocock, J., 1986: *Hegemony*. London: Tavistock.

Boddy, W., 2002: 'New media as old media: television', in D. Harries (ed.), *The New Media Book*. London: BFI, 242–53.

Blumler, J.E. and Katz, E.J., 1974: *The Uses of Mass Communication*. London: Sage.

Bolter, J.D. and Grusin, R., 2000: *Remediation: Understanding New Media*. Cambridge, Ma.: MIT Press.

Brenton, S. and Cohen, R., 2003: *Shooting People: Adventures in Reality TV*. New York: Verso.

Bruns, A., 2002: 'Resource centre sites: the new gatekeepers of the web?', PhD dissertation, University of Queensland.

Burnett, R. and Marshall, P.D., 2003: *Web Theory: an Introduction*. London: Routledge

Callois, R., 1979: *Man, Play, and Games*. Barash, M. (trans.). New York: Schoken.

Cassell, J. and Jenkins, H., 1998: *From Barbie to Mortal Kombat: Gender and Computer Games*. Cambridge, Ma.: MIT Press.

Castells, M., 1996: *The Rise of the Network Society: The Information Age: Economy, Society and Culture*, Vol. 1. Cambridge, Ma.: Blackwell.

Castells, M., 1997: *The Power of Identity*, Vol. II. Cambridge, Ma.: Blackwell.

Castells, M., 1998: *End of Millenium: The Information Age: Economy, Society and Culture*, Vol. 3. Cambridge, Ma.: Blackwell.

Chesher, C., 1996: 'CD-Rom's identity crisis', *Media International Australia* 81, August, 27–33.

Crawford, C., 2002: *The Art of Interactive Design*. San Francisco: No Starch Press.

Cubitt, S., 2002: 'Digital filming and special effects', in D. Harries (ed.), *The New Media Book*. London: BFI, 17–29.

Darley, A., 2000: *Visual Digital Culture: Surface Play and Spectacle in New Media Genres*. New York: Routledge.

De Certeau, M., 1984: *The Practice of Everyday Life*. Berkeley: University of California Press.

Dee, J., 2003: 'Playing mogul', *New York Times Magazine*, 21 December, 36–41, 52, 53, 66–8.

De Lauretis, T. and Heath, S. (eds), 1985: *The Cinematic Apparatus*. New York: St Martin's Press.

Deleuze, G. and Guattari, F., 1987: *A Thousand Plateaus*. Massumi, B. (trans.) Minneapolis: University of Minnesota Press.

Dovey, J., 2000: *Freakshow: First Person Media and Factual Television*. London: Pluto Press.

Du Gay, P., Hall, S., Janes, L., Mackay, L. and Negus, K., 1997: *Doing Cultural Studies: The Story of the Sony Walkman*. London: Sage.

Dyer, R., 1986: *Heavenly Bodies: Film Stars and Society*. New York: St Martin's Press.

Dyer-Witheford, N., 2002: 'E-capital and the many-headed Hydra', in G. Elmer (eds), *Critical Perspectives on the Internet*. Lanham, Maryland: Rowman & Littlefield.

Electronic Freedom Foundation, 2004: http://www.eff.org/ (February).

Ellul, J., 1964: *The Technological Society*. New York: Knopf.

Elmer, G. (ed.), 2002: *Critical Perspectives on the Internet*. Lanham, Maryland: Rowman & Littlefield.

Enzensberger, H.M., 1974: *The Consciousness Industry: On Literature, Politics and the Media*. New York: Seabury Press.

Erard, M., 2004: 'The ivy-covered console', *New York Times*, 26 February, E1, 6.

ESA (Entertainment Software Association), 2003: http://www.theesa.com/pressroom.html.

ESA (Entertainment Software Association), 2004: http://www.theesa.com/pressroom.html.

Europe Shareware, 2004: http://www.europe-shareware.org/pages/shareware.us.html (10 February).

E-vite, 2004: press release: http://www.evite.com/pages/gt/press/pressReleases/020404.jsp (February).

Ferkiss, V., 1969: *Technological Man: Myth and Reality*. London: Heinemann.

Fessenden, F., 2003: 'Slipping into a new shell', *New York Times*, Thursday 23 Oct., E1, 6.

Fiske, J., 1987: *Television Culture*. New York: Routledge/Methuen.

Fiske, J., 1989: *Understanding Popular Culture*. Boston: Unwin Hyman.

Fiske, J., 1996: *Media Matters: Everyday Culture and Political Change*. Minneapolis: University of Minnesota Press.

Fornas, J., Klein, K., Ladendorf, M., Ladendorf, S. and Sveningsson, M., 2002: *Digital Borderlands: Cultural Studies and Interactivity on the Internet*. New York: Peter Lang.

Forrester, 2004: online www.forrester.com.

Foucault, M., 1995: *Discipline and Punish: The Birth of the Prison*. New York: Vintage.

Free Software Foundation, 2003: 'The gnu manifesto', www.gnu.org/gnu/manifesto.html (October).

Gerbner, G. 1988: *Violence and Terror in the Mass Media*. Paris: Unesco.

Gere, C., 2002: *Digital Culture*. London: Reaktion Books.

Greenfeld, K.T., 2000: 'Meet the Napster/What's next for Napster?' *Time* 156: 14, 2 October, cover story.

Grodal, T., 2003: 'Stories for eye, ear, and muscles: video games, media and embodied experiences', in M.J.P. Wolff and B. Perron, *The Video Game Theory Reader*. London: Routledge, 129–55.

Grossberg, L., 1992: *We Gotta Get Out of This Place: Popular Conservatism and Postmodernism*. New York: Routledge.

Habermas, J., 1989: *The Structural Transformation of the Public Sphere*. Thomas Burger (trans.). Cambridge, Ma.: MIT Press.

Hall, S., 1978: 'Notes on deconstructing the "popular"', in R. Samuel (ed.), *People's History and Socialist Theory*. London: Routledge Kegan Paul.

Hall, S., 1981: 'Notes on Deconstructing the Popular' in Raphael Samuel (ed.), *People's History and Socialist Theory*. London: Routledge & Kegan Paul.

Haraway, D., 1991: *Simians, Cyborgs and Women: The Reinvention of Nature*. New York: Routledge.

Harries, D. (ed.), 2002: *The New Media Book*. London: BFI.

Harris, L., 2002: *The ifilm Internet Movie Guide*. Hollywood, Ca.: Lone Eagle Publishing.

Hartley, J., 1992: *The Politics of Pictures: The Creation of the Public in the Age of Popular Media*. London: Routledge.

Hayles, N.K., 1999: *How we Became Post-human: Virtual Bodies in Cybernetics, Literature and Informatics*. Chicago: Chicago University Press.

Hebdige, D., 1988: *Subculture: The Meaning of Style*. New York: Routledge.

Herman, L., 1997: *The Fall and Rise of Video Games* (2nd edn). Springfield, NJ: Rolenta Press.

Herold, 2003: 'A chase saga dominated by its cinematic cousin', *New York Times*, 15 May, E7.

Herz, J.C., 1997: *Joystick Nation: How Videogames Ate our Quarters, Won our Hearts, and Rewired our Minds*. Boston: Little, Brown and Co.

History of Film and Television, 2003: online: http://www.high-techproductions.com/historyoftelevision.htm.

Hoggart, R., 1957: *The Uses of Literacy: Aspects of Working-class Life with Special Reference to Publications and Entertainment*. Harmondsworth: Penguin.

Holson, L.M., 2003: 'Wrapping up a trilogy with a global assault', *New York Times*, 5 November, B1,10

Horkheimer, M. and Adorno, T.A., 1987: *The Dialectic of Enlightenment*. New York: Continuum.

Huizinga, J., 1955: *Homo Ludens: A Study of the Play Element in Culture*. Boston: Beacon Press.

IGDA 2003: 'Online games part two', online: http://www.digitalgamedeveloper.com/2003/04_apr/features/dligdawppt2.htm (15 October).

Innis, H.A., 1950: *Empire and Communication*. London: Oxford University Press.

Innis, H.A., 1951: *The Bias of Communication*. London: Oxford University Press.

Interactive Advertising Bureau, 2004: online: http://www.iab.net/news/pr2004524asp accessed May 26.

Interactivity Consultants, 2003: online: http://www.interactivityconsultants.com/pages/resources/interactivity_definition_and_ resources.htm.

Internet Movie Database, 2003: online: www.imdb.com http://imdb.com/Charts/usatopmovies.

Jenkins, H., 1992: *Textual Poachers: Television Fans and Participatory Culture*. New York: Routledge.

Kahney, L., 2003: 'Email mobs materialize all over', *Wired News*, 5 July, online: http://www.wired.com/news/culture/0,1284,59518,00.html.

Katz, E. and Lazarsfeld, P., 1955: *Personal Influence*. Glencoe, Ill.: Free Press.

Keller, J., 2002: 'Sopranos' finale goes bing!' E!Online, online: http://www.eonline.com/News/Items/0,1,10962,00.html, 11 December – accessed 30 April 2003.

Klein, N., 2000: *No Logo, No Space, No Choice, No Jobs: Taking Aim at the Brand Bullies*. London: Flamingo.

Kowal, D., 2002: 'Digitizing and globalizing indigenous voices: the zapatista movement', in G. Elmer (ed), *Critical Perspectives on the Internet*. Lanham, Maryland: Rowman & Littlefield, 105–26.

Kroker, A., 1984: *Technology and the Canadian Mind: Innis/McLuhan/Grant*, Montreal: New World Perspectives.

Kroker, A. and Weinstein, M.A., 1994: *Data Trash: The Theory of the Virtual Class*. New York: St Martin's Press.

Lahti, M., 2003: 'As we become machines: corporealized pleasures in video games', in M.J.P. Wolf, and B. Perron (eds), *The Video Game Theory Reader*. New York: Routledge, 157–70.

Leonhardt, D., 2003: 'A voice in the calling wilderness', *New York Times*, 18 Dec., E1, 8.

Levinson, P., 1999: *Digital McLuhan: A Guide to the Information Millennium*. New York: Routledge.

Lyotard, J.F., 1985: *The Postmodern Condition: A Report on Knowledge*. B. Massumi and G. Bennington (trans.). Minneapolis: University of Minnesota Press.

McLuhan, M., 1965: *Understanding Media: The Extensions of Man*. New York: McGraw-Hill.

Manovich, L., 2001: *The Language of New Media*. Cambridge, Ma: MIT Press.

Marcuse, H., 1964: *One Dimensional Man: Studies in the Ideology of Advanced Industrial Society*. Boston: Beacon Press.

Markham, A., 1998: *Life Online: Researching Real Experience in Virtual Space*. Walnut Creek, Ca: Atlantic Press/Sage.

Marriott, M., 2003: 'Theirs for the tweaking', *New York Times*, 4 Dec., E1, 4.

Marshall, P.D., 1997: 'The commodity and the internet: interactivity and the generation of the audience commodity', *Media International Australia*, February, 51–62.

Marshall, P.D., 2001: 'Video and computer gaming', in S. Cunningham and G. Turner (eds), *The Media and Communications in Australia* (3rd edn), Sydney: Allen and Unwin, 258–74.

Marshall, P.D., 2002: 'The new intertextual commodity', in D. Harries, *The New Media Book*. London: BFI, 69–81.

Massmog, 2003: 'A tale in the desert: release date and final beta session', online: www.massmog.com, posted 18 January.

Metz, Christian, 1982: *The Imaginary Signifier: Psychoanalysis and Cinema*. Bloomington, Indiana: Indiana University Press.

Miller, T., McMurria, J. and Maxwell, R., 2001: *Global Hollywood*. London: BFI.

Mittell, J., 2003: 'Interfacing television: TiVo, technology convergence and everyday life', Media in Transition: Television International Conference, MIT, May, online: http://cms.mit .edu/mit3/papers/Mittell.pdf.

Moran, A., 1998: *Copycat Television: Globalization, Programme Formats and Cultural Identity*. Luton: University of Luton Press.

Mumford, L., 1934: *Technics and Civilization*. London: Routledge Kegan Paul.

Murray, S. and Ouellette, L. (eds), 2004: *Reality Television: Remaking Television Culture*. New York: New York University Press.

Nielsen/Netratings, 2004: http://direct.www.nielsen-netratings.com/news.jsp?section=dat_gi, January.

O'Regan, T. and Goldsmith, B., 2002: 'Emerging ecologies of production', in D. Harries (ed.), *The New Media Book*. London: BFI, 92–105.

Oxford English Dictionary, 2002 [electronic resource]. Oxford: Oxford University Press.

Pargman, D., 2000: 'The fabric of virtual reality: courage, rewards and death in an adventure MUD', M/C – A Journal of Media and Culture, 3:5, online: www.mediaculture.org/0010/ mud.html.

Pew Internet and American Life Project, 2000: *Tracking Online Life: How Women Use the Internet to Cultivate Relationships with Family and Friends*. Washington, DC, online: www.pewinternet.org.

Pierson, M., 2002: *Special Effects: Still in Search of Wonder*. New York: Columbia University Press.

Pogue, D., 2003: 'Satellite radio extends its orbit', *New York Times*, Thursday, 18 Dec., E1, 9.

Poole, S., 2000: *Trigger Happy: The Inner Life of Videogames*. London: Fourth Estate.

Robbins, B. (ed.), 1993: *The Phantom Public Sphere*. Minneapolis, MI: University of Minnesota Press.

Rogers, E., 1995: *Diffusion of Innovations* (4th edn). New York: Free Press.

Schactman, N., 2004: 'Copyright enters a gray area', *Wired News*, 14 February, http://www. wired.com/news/digiwood/0,1412,62276,00.html?tw=wn_story_top5.

Shatkin, E., 2003: 'DG2L releases world's first MPEG-4 digital cinema system', *Digital Cinema Magazine*, 17 December, online: http://www.uemedia.net/CPC/digitalcinemamag/ article_5901.shtml.

Star Wars official website, 2004: www.starwars.com.

Swingewood, A., 1977: *The Myth of Mass Culture*. London: Macmillan.

TiVo, 2004: accessed online: http://a423.g.akama.net./7/423/1788/4b2936006f016d/www. tivo.com/pdfs/reports/Q4_FY04_release.pdf

Tulloch, J. and Jenkins, H., 1995: *Science Fiction Audiences: Watching Dr Who and Star Trek*. New York: Routledge.

Turkle, S., 1995: *Life on the Screen: Identity in the Age of the Internet*. New York: Simon & Schuster.

Turner, G., 1999: *Film as Social Practice*. London: Routledge.

Turner, G., 2002: *British Cultural Studies: An Introduction*. London: Routledge.

Wasko, J., 2002: 'The future of film distribution and exhibition', in D. Harries (ed.), *The New Media Book*. London: BFI, 195–206.

Wiener, N., 1948: *Cybernetics; Or, Control and Communication in the Animal and the Machine*. New York: Wiley.

Williams, A., 2002: 'MTV's *Real World*', *New York Magazine*, 19 December, online: http://www.newyorkmetro.com/nymetro/arts/tv/n_8081/.

Williams, R., 1958: *Culture and Society, 1780–1950*. London: Chatto & Windus.

Williams, R., 1965: *The Long Revolution*. Harmondsworth: Pelican.

Wilson, S., 'The aesthetics and practice of designing interactive computer events', http://userwww.sfsu.edu/~swilson/papers/interactive2.html.

Wolf, M.J.P. and Perron, B. (eds), 2003: *The Video Game Theory Reader*. New York: Routledge.

Wyatt, J., 1994: *High Concept: Movies and Marketing in Hollywood*. Austin: University of Texas Press.

Index